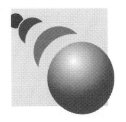

O U G H T E N
H O U S E
P U B L I C A T I O N S

"Ascension Books for the Rising Planetary Consciousness"

Bridge Into Light will give you some techniques and exercises which can assist you in connecting with your own higher wisdom and spiritual guidance. If you follow the guidelines set forth, you should have wonderful results. That which you experience in using the exercises in this book is uniquely for you. The authors and the publisher offer this information to you as a gift from Spirit, with the hope that it will assist you in your own development and personal ascension process. We assume no responsibility for the use of the materials.

We are each solely responsible for what we know, who we are, and how we act. This is just the way it is. The effects of the meditation exercises, the uses to which you put the knowledge gained, and what you experience is solely up to you, the reader. As humans, we are each ultimately responsible for our actions. We honor the sovereignty of each individual and the partnership that each one has with their own higher wisdom. We acknowledge that we each have our lessons to learn. As we honor this responsibility for each of you, we ask that you also honor it in the use of these materials and as you share what you have gained within these pages with others. That said, be encouraged to look through your own "opening doors" and see what awaits you on the other side!

A companion tape to *Bridge Into Light* is available through Oughten House Publications. This tape was also created by the Camerons and is based on the book. It follows the same step-by-step process for bridging the dimensions to connect with your own spiritual guidance. The meditations are accompanied by original music designed to enhance your experience.

Bridge Into Light

by

Pam Cameron

&

Fred Cameron

Oughten House Publications

Livermore, California

Bridge Into Light
Your Connection to Spiritual Guidance

EDITING & TYPOGRAPHY BY SARA BENJAMIN
COVER ILLUSTRATION BY CATHIE BEACH
PRINTED BY PATTERSON PRINTING, BENTON HARBOR, MICHIGAN

Published by:
Oughten House Publications
P.O. Box 2008
Livermore, California, 94551-2008 USA

Library of Congress Cataloging-in-Publication Data
Bridge into light : your connection to spiritual guidance;
Pam Cameron, Fred Cameron, -- 2nd ed.
     p.   cm.
     ISBN 1-880666-07-3 (alk. paper) : $11.95
     1. Channeling (Spiritualism). 2. Spiritual life -- Miscellanea. 3.
Ascended Masters. 4. Self -- Miscellanea. I. Cameron, Pam, 1945 –
II. Cameron, Fred, 1945 – .
BF1286,C35   1992
133.9'1--dc20   92-35243
                                              CIP
ISBN 1-880666-07-3, Trade Publication
Printed in United States of America
Printed on recycled paper

iv

I've come to speak with you about love — the kind of love which fills the heart until it expands, love which goes beyond the limits of your heart, love so great it would fill the room. That is the love of the Father for his children on the Earth. You know the essence of this love, but its magnitude is so vast, it is so light, it could sustain life. It could sustain you through trying times.

There is love all around, abounding. You see it on the wings of a bird, you see it in the tree, you see it in the smile of a child. If you could let this love fill you, it would come down from above and fill your being so that what shines out from your countenance is a reflection of this expanded heart. All who come near you will be touched by this love, be attracted to this love, and know this love.

What we want to do is to give people something to hang their hats on at this time of spiritual rebirth on the Earth. This rebirth is going to bring new information and philosophy. It is said that to enter the kingdom of heaven you must be innocent as a child, full of wonder and awe, and accept all that is around you. Unfortunately, once people have developed their beliefs, it is difficult for them to become childlike again. But now the information is so new and so incredible that all will be forced to have this childlike wonder when they hear it, because these ideas have never been heard before. How could you judge if they are right or wrong? They are new. They are simply new.

Once people believed the world was flat. Then there were those who suggested it was not. That was a preposterous idea at the time, but history tells us that [that] idea was correct and [that] those clinging to their old beliefs were simply unaware. That was a difficult time. We are now in a time of new growth and expanded awareness, once again. There will be those who insist there is nothing beyond the third dimension. But in this lifetime it will be proven that there is more to reality than man has believed in the past.

— Sananda

→→ ACKNOWLEDGMENTS ←←

The authors would like to thank the Masters for their guidance and support in creating this book. Archangel Michael, Lord Jesus-Sananda, Ashtar, Kuthumi, and Archangel Gabriel have been our steadfast guidance in putting together these exercises.

We would also like to acknowledge Rev. Cathie Beach for allowing us to include the Hilarion healing meditation and for the cover artwork which she channeled, and Eric and Christine Klein for their commitment to this work and for allowing us to include the channeled Light Pyramid and Violet Flame exercises. Finally, many thanks to our editor, Sara Benjamin, for making this a better book.

✦ TABLE OF CONTENTS ✦

→ LIST OF EXERCISES ←

⤞ Introduction ⤝

There are momentous events now occurring, things that have never before happened in recorded history. These events are outside of us in the world, and inside of us in our innermost selves. There are Earth changes and weather extremes: more earthquakes, more drought, more flooding. The inner changes that many of us are experiencing are more subtle, but just as real. Many people are receiving "wake up" calls that are intensely personal during this time of unprecedented spiritual awakening.

Spiritual energies, or beings, are making themselves known to an increasing number of people — in fact to all who are willing to listen. The message is profound: It is time to wake up those parts of yourself that have been asleep, those parts which are open to experiencing wonder, those parts which question "why," those parts which reason without limitation. This message sparks the innocence and imagination which were born within each of us, and awakens our own innate wisdom. It is an awareness of the vastness of the Source from which we came. It is our connection to Spirit. These are the parts of us that know there is more to life than what we see on television, more than we experience in our jobs, more even than we experience in our relationships. For in the midst of our often hectic lifestyles, the quiet spaces required to allow the inner knowing to emerge are rare.

Because we are so accustomed to receiving our information from external sources, these inner messages are often faint, and we sometimes question whether they are real. What does seem real are the things which we can see with our eyes and hear with our ears, the things which are validated by the physical world and by others around us.

But we have always received inner messages. We called them hunches, intuition, or feelings. These messages are our guidance. They are the fulfillment of our inner longing to *know*. What is different today is that these messages are growing stronger. They can no longer be brushed off because they seem "unscientific" or "unreal," because there is a compelling urgency about the call to listen. Our inner voice deserves to be heard and acted upon, just as does the voice of Mother Nature.

For those already tuned in to their own knowing, these messages are loud and clear. For those who yearn to hear, there is a way to strengthen the ability to receive their own unique guidance. The purpose of this book is to assist all who desire to receive knowledge and guidance *directly*, to do so. This means there would be direct communication between that highest part of your self and the conscious part of your self.

We have assembled a series of exercises (which we have received in this direct manner) from many spiritual beings who have assisted us in this endeavor. It is with their guidance and support that we have been able to make the leap of faith out of our comfort zones to bring you their messages.

They have presented methods whereby each of us can awaken to our own inner guidance.

These exercises are designed to help you open your mind to your own sources of knowledge. We do not presume to know what messages may be communicated to you once you are open to them and have learned to hear them. We do know, however, that the spirit of the messages will be in loving support and guidance for your highest good, and that they will be presented in a way which will be most meaningful to you.

We know there will be many questions and that we will only begin to answer them. What we hope to do is to show you how to open the door so that you will begin to see. It is your task to do the actual opening and to discover for yourself what is on the other side of the door.

In this book, we present exercises which will give you the opportunity to communicate with these Masters yourself. It is not difficult, as they are showering urgent messages upon all who will but take the time to listen. They are calling us in an attempt to wake us up to our true nature. We are not just human beings with short life spans; we are also magnificent beings of Light.

If you are looking, or longing, for something better in your life, and if you know that it is very close if you could only understand it, then perhaps you will decide to try these exercises. We offer no religion, no philosophy, no "answers." These are for you to find on your own. We only offer some techniques to help you hear the wisdom that is already coming to you from higher sources.

The intensity and success of these exercises can be enhanced by doing them in groups. Even two people doing the exercises together can have a profound effect on the results. We ask only that you let yourself believe that they will work for you. If some of the concepts we present seem strange, if some of the beings we describe are unfamiliar — even if you don't think they really "exist" — we ask that you set aside skepticism until you have reached the point where you can truly decide for yourself.

In our case, we had no past experience with anything like this. Our reasoning said "We are a computer programmer and a businesswoman." But our hearts said "We know this is right," and, indeed, it felt right in the deepest parts of us. We wrote this book to build a bridge between realities. Our intent is to shine a light so that others might see the way to cross that bridge and connect with the spiritual parts of themselves.

No other person can convince you that these ideas are true or false. You must use your own reasoning powers. You must be open to the feelings from your heart and you must finally decide on your own, for only in your own heart lies the truth. You have only to learn to listen.

CHAPTER ONE

Ascension and Light

Spiritual awakening often requires a traumatic event to create an opening. The October 1989 Loma Prieta earthquake in California was just such an event for us. We experienced the earthquake in its full intensity, as our home was but a few short miles from the epicenter. Feeling the greatness of nature's power had a profound effect: our very foundations were shaken, both physically and emotionally. The experience of the earthquake caused suppressed feelings to surface and many people made dramatic changes in their lives as a result.

Shortly after the earthquake, while we were still experiencing daily aftershocks, Fred sensed an urgency to move away from the uncertainties of living on a fault zone. While walking one day, with all of these experiences and upcoming decisions ever-present in her mind, the thought popped into Pam's head, "What you need to do is to get ready to ascend." The message came from within. It was quite clear and, although Pam didn't really know what it meant, she had a compelling feeling that it was important. So — months later — when a friend invited her to go listen to someone channeling information about ascension, she knew instantly she had to be there to find out more.

In this book we will share with you what we have learned, all beginning with the spark of that one fleeting thought. That spark has grown into a flame — kindled by information and experience, and then allowed to expand as our beliefs and our horizons also expanded.

And so it is with each one. Awareness of ascension comes in often subtle, always personal ways. Hopefully, everyone will not require the earth to move, but many will have dramatic wake-up calls as the Earth changes continue. Part of the purpose of these changes is to create an opportunity for many people to take a deeper look at their values and to become more connected to Spirit quickly, for there is an urgency to man's awakening.

Approaching Change

As we view the world around us, many changes are apparent, with more happening all the time. There have been political changes: Germany is reunited and the Berlin Wall is down; dictators have been overthrown in Nicaragua and Czechoslovakia; the USSR no longer exists. There have already been climatic changes, earthquakes around the world, floods and droughts, rain forests that are disappearing, holes in the ozone layer. The globe is either warming or cooling, depending on which scientist you ask. ·

You may be changing too, partly as a response to these outside changes, but also in response to inner feelings: an increasing dissatisfaction with old ways of being that don't seem to work any more and a growing interest in other things that may or may not be familiar to you.

Some of the inner changes occurring now are the result of new information from the heavens that is being showered upon the Earth and her beings. Indeed, some of this information will cause us all to rethink and expand our concepts of reality in order to encompass the new ideas.

New concepts require a new frame of reference, maybe even a new way of viewing the world. This kind of change is referred to as a paradigm shift. Your "paradigm" is your view of the world and changing it is something like crossing a bridge. Standing on one side you are able to look around and see what is there. You may have some idea of what is on the other side. But, once the bridge is crossed, you become aware of things which you didn't have any idea existed before. With this new information, your view of reality is expanded and your perceptions are permanently changed. We can experience this kind of shift personally, as life brings us new experiences and awareness. It can also occur globally, as events or changes create new views of reality for mankind.

At first, a new reality has to be described in existing terms to be understood. As an example, there was a paradigm shift when the automobile was invented. Before cars, there were horses and carriages. People didn't know what to call this new invention, so a name was used which everyone could relate to from current terminology: the horseless carriage.

An even more significant paradigm shift occurred when man discovered that the Earth was not flat. Can you imagine how greatly mankind's thinking had to change to fully comprehend this new concept? Our entire view of reality had to change. How many events can you think of in your lifetime that have created this kind of shift in perception?

As we begin to discuss new ideas and concepts, your current views of reality will be challenged. But just as you could walk around a "horseless carriage" and kick the tires, just as Columbus could sail to the New World without falling off the edge, so you will be able to test these new concepts and determine whether or not they belong in your reality. All you need is an open mind, an open heart, and a willingness to take time for discovery. Then you will know directly; no authorities, no writers (including us), will be necessary for you to know.

About Dimensions

We will acknowledge that our philosophers, physicists, mathematicians, and the rest of us do not understand dimensions, so these terms cannot be discussed with any general agreement. However, we will give you the understanding we have received from our guides, so that we can at least have a mutual frame of reference.

The third dimension refers to our physical existence as we currently know it on Earth. It includes all those things which are perceived with the five physical senses. The very nature of the third dimension limits our ability to perceive the rest of creation.

The fourth dimension is the astral plane, where souls caught on the wheel of reincarnation may go when death of the body occurs. Ascension will give each of us the opportunity to move off of the wheel and bypass this dimension, moving directly on to the higher dimensions.

The fifth dimension is that plane of existence where we go when we ascend. It is a dimension of timelessness and love. This means that time ceases to be linear and thoughts manifest as reality almost immediately. The Ascended Masters say it is a place where the Light and Love of God are more intense and direct than they are in the third dimension. It is a place where God's "volume" is turned up. A part of us sometimes visits the fifth dimension when we have a pleasant dream. It is a place where a part of us already exists, the part we call the Higher Self.

Although we refer to the fifth dimension as a place, it can also be thought of as a state of being. We cannot simply go there or achieve this state without some preparation which will shift our way of being. For example, in our world there are many professions which require extensive training before one is able to practice them. You may not perform as a surgeon without having earned the credentials and gained sufficient experience. Likewise, there are things we cannot do until we have gained the required skills, such as earning a place on an Olympic track team or completing a difficult technical climb to the top of a sheer cliff. In a similar way, the fifth dimension cannot be reached without having developed a certain quality of being. We are simply not given the ability to exist in that place without first developing a "lightness of being," a *body of light* that will sustain us there.

About Light

The fifth dimension is a dimension of light. But, unlike our world where light just seems to illuminate and warm material things, "real light" and "bodies of light" are the visible substance of the fifth dimension.

Despite the pronouncements of our scientists, this is a spiritual universe, and the requirements for creating our bodies of light are spiritual in nature. However, unlike the person who would like to run the mile on an Olympic track team but who will never have the physical ability, all of us have the same strength and the same potential for obtaining a Light Body. Regardless of our race, sex, religious beliefs, or financial status, we all have the same unfailing inner God as a guide and the same potential for discovering that our Light Bodies are already a part of us now.

You will need to *lighten* yourself in preparation for becoming a fifth-dimensional being. This lightening occurs as you cast off your weights and burdens and as you expand your limits to include a closer connection to your Creator. This is the true meaning of the word "en*light*enment," which is no longer for the few but now is for the many.

Ascension

The message of ascension is *love*; the method is *light*. As we begin our ascension processes and accept our own personal divinity, we gain a sense of wholeness heretofore unknown. By casting off emotional burdens, we will become lighter and more able to fully and completely love ourselves and others. This lightness is a requirement for ascension.

The work of building a body of light is called the process of *ascension*. The energy vibrations in your body will be raised and, at some point in this process, your existence can shift into a higher dimension. When this occurs, your quality of being will have "lightened" to the extent that you will be able to choose to move to the fifth and higher dimensions — to choose to ascend.

This is the choice that is being given to each person at this time. Choose to open your hearts to God's guidance by first loving yourself, and then all others, without qualification. Then you may ascend to the fifth dimension where these qualities are a requirement of being.

Ascension is a healing process, as well as a transformational one, for both mankind and Earth. It is a process which culminates in a physical and spiritual transformation. In the past, there have been beings who ascended to the fifth dimension instead of dying. They were *lifted* to a place where the cycles of life, death, and rebirth do not occur. Many of them returned as *ascended beings*, walking and living on this Earth. Now this ascension process will occur much more often. We will ascend with our bodies and without dying. This is God's Grace for these new times.

Reunion with God has been the ultimate goal of nearly every religion since time began. This union has been called *nirvana* by the Buddhists, ascension (or The Rapture) by Christians and others. Preparing for it is a process through which you develop an acceptance of your own personal divinity so that illusions of limitation no longer exist. You come to accept your personal power for manifestation, and understand your connection to the Divine Source and to your fellow man. As this connection to the spiritual parts of your self becomes more integrated and balanced with those other aspects of your self, you will become more whole and more fully who you were always meant to be.

When Jesus Christ ascended, this same lifting was promised as a possibility for all of mankind. We are not required to actually live the type of life that Buddha or Jesus lived. We are only required to sincerely desire it in our hearts. Once we begin to do this, we will naturally change our attitudes and our very natures. In doing so, our indwelling God will begin to construct the Body of Light that will take us to the higher dimensions.

You will probably have many questions about what we are proposing. In this book we hope to give you the tools to receive your own answers directly. We also had questions and will share some of the answers we have received. We hope you may feel encouraged to begin, knowing that the effort and the changes required will be worthwhile.

Any person who wishes to may ascend. This has always been an option to every human, although few have known this in times past. At the present time, ideas about God are so confused, so mixed up and misleading, that Spirit's best approach is to try to reach every single person directly. That is what is happening at this time of global awakening. Messages from Spirit are beginning to pierce the veil which has separated mankind from the higher dimensions for so long, and humanity is being granted new and clearer understandings directly.

Messages received directly from Spirit have more impact because they are not diluted by repetition and interpretation; they are much harder to ignore because they arrive through personal experience and are very real. They lead to a keen sense of knowing. Many people will not be open to these messages at this time. But, later on, many more people will be awakened when those beings who have already ascended visibly reveal themselves and demonstrate the truth of these ideas.

The Earth and The Miracle

The Earth is also going to ascend, as one great cycle is ending and another is beginning. This will be a cleansing and purifying process for our planet. There are many prophecies pointing to this time. They can be found in the Mayan calendar, in the messages encoded in the Great Pyramid in Egypt, in the book of Revelation in the Bible, in the prophecies of Nostradamus, in the legends of the Hopi Indians, in the teachings of Edgar Cayce and many others.

They all talk about a time when dramatic Earth changes will occur. It is not given to mankind to know when this will happen, or exactly what form it will take. Only God knows this. Nor is it given to man to alter the course the Earth is taking.

What is being given to all of us now on Earth — without exception — is a special dispensation from God. This is the miracle. We are being offered the loving assistance of beings who exist in the fifth and higher dimensions. They are giving methods, encouragement, and a path to all of us, so we can begin our ascension process as the Earth begins hers, so we will be prepared to live in harmony with each other in the new age.

Some may regard the ascension as the ending — the ending of an age. More importantly, it marks the beginning of a new age for mankind and for the planet. We are already moving into this new age — gradually, step by step. But, as we each must make a leap upward to come into our new awareness and being, so must Earth make a leap to her new dimension.

The fact of Earth's ascension will be at the center of many of the individual choices we each will be making in the coming years. The miracle is that each of us can receive direct guidance, which will help us to understand what the Earth changes mean and to make choices for our own highest good.

Belief and Acting "As If"

Right now, you may be thinking, "This is all very interesting, but I have no experience with anything of the kind. I can't really believe this is true." So you go back to your jobs and your life, affected a little, changed a little, but not convinced.

And yet ... there is something nagging about all this. There is a corner of your mind that thinks: Suppose this is true? Suppose this ascension applies to me, as they say it does? Suppose, for a while, I don't ignore it; what would happen? Suppose I tried some of the exercises to see for myself what might happen? Suppose I could have an Ascended Master talk directly to me? At least then I would know firsthand whether any of this is true, without having to believe what someone else says.

The exercises in this book are designed to help you see for yourself: they are designed to allow you to open yourself sufficiently to receive this communication. You must be able to suspend your disbelief for a time to accept what we are saying, to act as if it were true. It is like going to a movie. For example, we know that every character in the movie *E.T.* is fictional. At one level, we know that a boy did not befriend an alien from a spaceship and hide him in his bedroom closet. Yet, on another level, we so completely accept the story, we are so touched by the apparent death of E.T. and the distress of the other characters, that we are moved to tears. We bought posters and T-shirts that said, "E.T. Phone Home!" So many of us were affected that we made *E.T.* one of the most popular films ever made.

We know we may be asking you to change your view of reality. But we also ask that you honor that part of yourself where your imagination lies. Allow yourself to close your eyes and take a splendid series of trips with these exercises. Allow yourself to "phone home" and listen to the message on the other end. It is quite beautiful.

Chapter Two

Beings of Light

Spiritual Beings

Over a period of many months — at first in our meditations and later on in our channelings — we became increasingly aware that there really do exist many types of beings, in planes of existence that are very different from our own.

First, let us make explicit what types of beings we are *not* discussing. This book does not deal with supposed "aliens" in UFOs, nor does it deal with "departed spirits." Nor will we be concerned with other physical planets or the "astral plane."

The spiritual beings that we will describe all wish to help you strengthen your bridge of communication to them. At this time of transformation, they come to lovingly assist all of us who will listen. They have had much practice doing this, for their function is, indeed, service to others in all things. These spiritual beings are beings of Light. When you visualize yourself wrapped in a vibrant white light of protection, you are manifesting some of that spiritual light. As your awareness of your oneness with Spirit grows, this light within you expands and you begin to grow more into your own body of light. You will be emerging into your own Light Body.

Of course, none of us knows — from books, religion, society, science, or our friends — whether spiritual beings really exist or not. We cannot see them. Nonetheless, there are many other things that we cannot see that we know are quite real. We cannot see the air we breathe (when it's clear outside), yet we know it sustains our life. It is the particles floating in the air that we see and smell: flower pollen, smog, perfume, cooking aromas. We cannot see electricity, magnetism, gravity, or radio waves, yet we know they are real. Each time we turn on our radios or television sets we experience the effects of these unseen energies.

More to the point, we cannot see our emotions and feelings. But lest you think these are unreal, consider how you would feel if you saw an angry parent strike a child in the face. Hard. So hard, the child fell down crying. Certainly this would be an ugly event, but the emotions you would experience in your heart upon witnessing it are much more direct and more powerful than any rational thoughts you might have about such an incident. We can't see feelings, but they are real and they flow among us constantly.

Once you admit that it is possible that spiritual beings might exist and the longing arises for more evidence, you have taken the first step required to expand your understanding of reality. The exercises later in this book will give you the tools to find out for yourself. For now, we will posit that angels and other spiritual beings do, indeed, exist as forms of energy, and we will share some of what our experience has taught us about them.

Who Are We?

Everything is made of energy. Some of this energy is very dense and manifests in our world as physical matter — our physical bodies, for example. Other parts of this energy are less dense, lighter, and do not manifest to our normal senses in the same way. We cannot usually perceive these subtle energies nor measure them with our current instruments. However, that does not mean they do not exist.

The physical body is surrounded by several energy bodies that most of us cannot see. Each body is surrounded by the next, similar to Chinese nesting boxes. We each have an emotional body and a mental body, among others. It is sufficient for our purposes to say that these bodies are interconnected, and that changes in one body will cause changes in another. It is becoming an accepted belief that much disease is caused by emotions which have been held in the body for an extended period of time. For example, when emotions such as anger or fear have sustained themselves for a prolonged time, an imbalance is created which will ultimately have an effect on the physical body.

From the perspective of our conscious minds, it is difficult (but not impossible) to be aware of the "lighter" parts of our beings. This awareness must come from inner effort and attention; it is by cultivating an inner awareness through meditation that the gateway to our hidden selves can be approached and our spiritual bodies can begin to emerge. These ideas do not seem at all extreme when we consider how many things in the world we cannot see that we are perfectly sure exist.

There are other types of things that only a few people have seen, and the rest of us take on faith. Antarctica is a good example. After enough circumstantial evidence from others, and enough reinforcement, we all have come to believe that Antarctica really exists and that we could go there some day if we chose to. Another example is the sensation and reality of being in the Space Shuttle, two hundred miles above the Earth. We have seen man in weightless conditions through the eye of a camera, but we can't really know what it's like unless we also become astronauts so we can go and see for ourselves.

This book takes the "going there" approach of reaching for higher dimensions. In this chapter we will introduce you to the concept of your Higher Self and to beings of light who are trying to help you "get there."

Your Higher Self

Your Higher Self is a non-physical but potentially know-able part of *you*. It is your link to God, the link between the denser form of energy of the physical body and the Creator. There is a cord which is your permanent connection to God. This connection, which is woven of silver etheric thread, runs through the Higher Self.

Your Higher Self is not separate from you, even though you may often feel detached from it. Your deeds and actions do not determine how far it is from you, nor does distance matter in a linear sense. Indeed, your Higher Self will become a very real part of your experience as you integrate more fully with it.

Understand that your Higher Self can always be called upon for guidance. Information is filtered, interpreted, and brought to you through your Higher Self. It is your own personal source of knowing. The more attuned you are to your Higher Self, the more your deeds and actions will naturally be in alignment with it. As you become more integrated with your Higher Self, the more you will align with Divine Will.

At this time, everyone's connection to God (through the Higher Self) has been strengthened. This means that coming into alignment with Divine Will is easier now than it has ever been before. Your Higher Self is your inspiration, your imagination, your connection to God. Although you cannot see it, it is your intuition, your inner voice, and your guidance.

It is through meditation that you can become more attuned to, and more clearly understand, your connection to your Higher Self. Remember that it is always your intention that counts. If you desire this connection to become more known to you and you consciously state this desire, you will begin to feel more integrated. You will begin to realize that you and your Higher Self are actually two sides of the same coin. The feeling of separation will diminish until the coin turns into a clear lens. You will eventually realize that your Higher Self is no farther away than the front of a piece of paper is to its back. You will begin to realize that you are a divine and powerful being, capable of great service to yourself and others.

Cosmic Names

Each one of us has a name which is associated with our Higher Self or our spiritual essence. This name is usually different than our given name. It is the name which reflects our true essence, a name which carries a higher vibration and which we resonate with in higher dimensions.

This name is often called your cosmic name. It is a name you may take upon your ascension. Your cosmic name is an important part of you. When you learn this name and become familiar with it, you will begin to resonate with it. You will feel its vibration deep within you when it is spoken and know within your heart that it is correct.

The manner in which a cosmic name is received will be unique for each person. It may be revealed to you during your meditation. You may see letters spell it out in your mind's eye. You may hear your name. It may start with just the sound of the first letter or the first syllable, and then expand until it keeps running through your mind like a familiar tune. Although it is possible for someone else to find your name for you, each person should have the joy of discovering their own name from their own higher guidance. If you want to know your cosmic name, we encourage you to be quiet and go within and ask for it to be given directly to you.

Beings who have already ascended have received their cosmic names, and may prefer to use them in their communications, just as you may prefer to use your cosmic name at the appropriate time. We often use cosmic names throughout this book, as that is how many of our guides refer to themselves.

Angels

There are angels among us! They are with all of us. They are not distant, celestial beings, up in the heavens floating around. They are present. They are by our sides. They are blowing their horns and trying to wake up many. Great multitudes of angels have been called into service and are surrounding this planet to offer their assistance and support.

Angels are one of your connections to the Divine Light. Their purpose is to guide and to protect you — each one of you. If you are having difficulty hearing your guidance, ask the angels to raise you above your day-to-day duties and tasks for a little while. It is in these moments that you can receive guidance, either verbally or through your feelings and hunches. This is a way that you can use your own inner guidance to keep you going straight down the path of Light. In your meditations you can take a pause, get your bearings, and see what the angels are saying to you.

Each and every person has their own special guardian angel. You can discover yours, if you will but take the time. You can also call upon the major angels (called archangels), each representing the embodiment of a virtue or certain attributes of Spirit. Archangel Gabriel and Archangel Michael worked with us on the development of this book.

Archangel Gabriel

Archangel Gabriel is the herald of the new age. He is generally considered the most famous messenger of God. Archangel Gabriel is usually portrayed carrying a trumpet as a symbol of the work he performs. He serves mankind by resurrecting the latent powers of hope within individuals.

After asking for assistance with this section of the book, we received the following message from Archangel Gabriel:

We are called the heavenly host. Unfortunately, that gives you a misconception because indeed we are not off somewhere in the heavens. We are with you, we surround you, we watch over you — we are very close. Now, doesn't that make you feel good? We are your invisible guardians. We know your cares, your burdens, and your joys. We whisper gently in your ear and guide you on your path.

We are love. If each one knew — if they could see us and knew that they were surrounded with such caring and love —

how could there be so much sadness? People often believe in angels as if they were a fairy tale, but, indeed, we are very real etheric energies. What is man but a bundle of energy? It is just bundled in a denser form. Do you know that the lighter you become, the easier it is for you to see and feel the angels, because you are more like them?

As loving guides, we can shield you with our wings. I know what is in your heart before the words are spoken. The angels are much more interested in mankind than they are in flying around in the skies. We are really quite close. We can drift in and out of your awareness like the vapor of a cloud which seems to suddenly appear or disappear.

Archangel Michael

Archangel Michael is quite a magnificent being. He is known as the archangel of protection and deliverance. He carries a powerful and swift sword of blue flame which is made of the Light of God. This sword can be called upon to help you sever your self-imposed psychic ties to perceived limitations and attachments, and to lend you protection from outside influences.

I am the protector of souls. I have been operating for a very long time, longer than your world has been around. I have the Light of the Lord. I am the link and the transfer point from the unknown magnitude of God to worlds such as your own. I give to all that which they ask for. I speak to all who will listen, as you might listen to those who speak to you. We are all as interested in your world now as you might imagine an anxious father might be with his wife about ready to give birth. He knows that everything will turn out fine, but he knows the birth process may be a little painful. But it does not last long and soon mother and new child are doing well, growing and thriving. So, that is where we are. We know that everything will turn out well, and we come to offer you a way to release your pain. We are inviting you to come and be with us to begin, or to resume, your careers of service. I can arrange protection. I can help join you to what you desire, just as I can distance and separate you from that which you do not desire.

Ascended Masters

There are beings who have completed their lessons on Earth and who have already made the step to the fifth dimension, where they reside closer to God. Some are in physical form at this time and some are not. Each has a specific role to play in the Divine Plan, just as each person has a role to play on earth. The Ascended Masters are working for the Light under the guidance of the Ascended Master Sananda. They are the messengers of the Creator, attempting to awaken as many humans as possible in a very short time. The purpose of their "wake-up" calls is to remind us of our true natures: we are beings of Light and Love.

It was only through direct, personal experience that we were convinced that there are other dimensions to our universe, and that these Ascended Masters really do exist. They already exist in a dimension of timelessness and love, where you will also come to exist after your ascension.

Through these beings (who have great love for all human beings and for the Earth itself), love and energy are being transmitting to the Earth with unprecedented intensity. This support is being extended to those on the Earth at this time to assist them to make the transition in consciousness required to move forward into the new age. This love and energy is available to everyone.

These Ascended Masters have been a source of guidance and inspiration for this book and we would like to introduce them to you as they introduced themselves to us:

Sananda

When Sananda walked upon the Earth, he was known to many by the name of Jesus. He is well known as one of the greatest teachers of all time. Sananda comes to us now with none of the political or religious connotations that were attributed to him during and after his time on Earth. Quite the contrary: he is personal, up-to-date in every way, even humorous. His words, which are being received by many now, are modern and relevant. From his communications, we know he has quietly revisited our world many times during natural disasters, giving aid and comfort to those in need. He comes for all men, all women, and all children of the Earth. He comes for people of all religions and for people of no religion. When we talk to him, he hears our words and — in the quiet spaces in our lives — we can hear his words as well:

I can help you to become more divine, to follow the guidance of the Father, for that is my mission. It was my mission on Earth; it continues to be my mission now. But where I am now I can touch many. I can shower down my love straight to the hearts of many in a moment. The heart which is like stone can be softened; the heart which is like ice can be melted — and it happens with a wave of loving energy which can pass over and through a room and then stop to rest with individual beings.

You also can assist to spread this word of loving energy. You can send it forth until it surrounds the planet — a blanket of loving and peaceful energy settling down like a morning dew. You can direct this loving energy. Once you have made it a part of you, it will radiate from you like warmth radiates from the sun. You will learn to direct it and will be able to focus it on peace for the planet and for your homes. Protect your families with love.

Sananda counsels many of the spiritual beings who invisibly surround the Earth and are ready to assist all of us. They look to him for guidance and are working closely under his direction. It is under his masterful and loving guidance that we all have the opportunity to grow and learn at this critical time in Earth's history.

Saint Germain

Saint Germain is best known for the violet flames of transmutation and purification. When we speak the request and visualize the violet flames, he will assist in dissolving away and eliminating our burdens:

I am always happy to lend assistance when it is asked for. Much of the work that I do is to assist with enlightenment, with lightening. I am best known for the violet flames of transmutation which I use to help eliminate and disperse the burdens of mankind — the emotional burdens which keep him from lightness. It is not enough to cast off the burdens and drop them by the way and leave them lingering about in the universe. So I bring my violet flames and — when one is willing to release — I take that energy and simply dissolve it away. When you call upon the violet flames, you will be amazed at how effective they are.

Kuthumi

When Kuthumi lived on Earth he was known as the Apostle John. He was close to Jesus then and continues to work closely with him in the heavens. Kuthumi is of particular assistance in learning how to become open to Spirit and how to channel.

We send you our love and support. We ask that you trust us even when you are dealing with your struggles of physical survival. Know that your physical world is only a part of reality. There are other dimensions and your spiritual existence transcends the physical. It makes it easier to trust when you feel so connected to the Divine Plan.

The time you take to be in connection with higher information is well spent. Every day, please do this. Then you can go forth focused.

Make time. Make time for joy.

Make time for quietness.

Be in the moment.

Peace be with you.

Kuan Yin

Kuan Yin is known as the ancient oriental Mother-Goddess of Mercy who has been admired for countless ages. Her name means "She who hears prayers." She is another Ascended Master who lends assistance in both physical and emotional healing. She comes to us as a soft and gentle presence full of love and compassion. Her symbol is the unfolding lotus blossom.

I am Kuan Yin, beloved Mother-Goddess. I bring healing for the emotional body, for spirit. I can help with the healing for the physical body as well, but primarily my responsibilities are healing for the emotional body. That's where the pain begins; it only later manifests itself in the physical body. So when you call on me to work with you, I go to the heart of the problem, you might say.

I help to lift your energies, and with this lifting comes healing. It is the weight that causes a burden on your shoulders and on your soul, and part of the process of lightening is to release these burdens.

Ashtar

Ashtar is working under the direction of Sananda, assisting in the ascension processes of Earth and all mankind. He is the administrative and logistical commander of thousands of beings who are watching over us, who are healing us, who are offering us their assistance, and who will aid us in our individual ascension processes. Ashtar has much specific information for us that is very timely. In his own words:

I am Ashtar, commander of this great exercise which is about to occur on this your planet Earth. I was not incarnated on the Earth in times past. I come from a neighboring world which was similar to your world, and went through processes that were similar to your evolution and your ascension. This did not occur on your world but in a different world, somewhat close to your system.

I am the commander of many, but we do not like to be distinguished as some ones on your planet like to be distinguished. We work in a closer brotherhood than humans are used to. There are many interconnections among us and many different types of beings. The differences are not so pronounced as they are even among the different races and languages on your planet, because we all speak the same language, at least. We care not how we look to each other.

I assist and direct agents from many different places in the universe. There are many spiritual beings on and about the planet Earth and they do need some administration as they all partake of the energy of the Father. This is a very decentralized operation, and even those who are not proximate to each other find it very easy to work in harmony and do not work at cross purposes.

Serapis Bey

Serapis Bey is the keeper of the ascension flame and is known as "the great disciplinarian." His primary task is helping people prepare for the ascension process.

I have come to help you with your healing and to assist you with your own personal ascension path. The work you must do to prepare yourself is much more internal than external. So, when you call on me and I come to work with you, much of the work is for your emotional body. To lighten, that is my job — lightening. A shaking loose of the weights. And as you become lighter and lighter, you become a shining light, a Light Being. As the light shines out from you, others around you will be touched by it. I will give you oil for your lamp, oil to help it burn more brightly as the old densities are melted away. You will radiate this light until a feeling of joy fills your being — joy because you know you are becoming closer and closer to God.

Call on me and I will give you a sign, a physical sensation. Make a time and a place to sit in meditation. The connections which always have been there are becoming known to you. The main thing which is required is a desire and a willingness to commit the time to be still, to focus on your own divinity, for you are a Divine Being.

All of these Masters are working together and all of them are available to work with each of us. Their guidance is often profound and usually verifies our own inner wisdom. We would like to emphasize that no matter what guidance you receive, you always have free will to choose what actions you take. The Ascended Masters will never force you to do anything. They are available for guidance and support only. You make the choice to listen and only you can choose for yourself what you will do. You cannot choose for another, ever. The Masters respect this universal rule for themselves and ask that you honor it as well.

CHAPTER THREE

Going Within

We humans can, and do, communicate with spiritual beings. We can listen to their messages and guidance concerning our questions. In times past this communication was called prayer. In recent decades it has been called meditation, and more recently yet, channeling. Although there are differences, each of these are forms of direct communication with internal wisdom or "higher" guidance.

Know that our world has changed in the last few years, largely because of influences we cannot see. The Ascended Masters understand why these changes are occurring. If you wish to know firsthand why the weather is changing, for example, or why certain political events are happening, or why you are changing, then we ask that you open yourself and quiet yourself long enough to hear. Then, afterwards, think about what you have learned. When you are skilled enough through practice, ask specific questions and you will receive specific answers. The Masters are trying to give us information; all we have to do is listen.

There is a famous Zen story about a western philosopher who visited a Zen master with the intent of expounding his theories. During tea, the master listened to the philosopher and, while refilling his teacup, the master let the tea overflow until the philosopher exclaimed, "Stop, my teacup is full!" The master replied, "Yes, it is. But if you wish to learn something, you must first empty your cup so that new tea may be poured in."

Likewise, if you can empty your "cup" of your attachments, your assumptions, and your negative emotions, then God's love can be poured in. If you can empty yourself of preconceived ideas, limiting or limited beliefs, and be open to new ideas, you may be surprised at the newness and wonder you find.

Meditation is going within and quieting your mind so that you can be in direct communion with your inner self — that part of yourself that you do not generally experience in your day-to-day activities. Meditation is an attempt to still or distract the conscious stream of thoughts and images that arise in your minds, often unbidden. When this happens, you have access to the quieter, more receptive areas of your mind.

The meditation exercises are designed to help you enter a receptive state of consciousness so that you will be open to learn from your own inner guidance, your higher guidance. If you already meditate regularly, you may simply add these exercises to your practice. If you are new to meditation, the exercises will quickly get you started. As with any new skill, the more you practice, the sooner you will get results and the more profound the results will be.

If you are new to meditation and you are not sure you can get any results (perhaps because you have tried before and you felt nothing happened) we suggest you act as if something *is* happening. You are not going to go into a trance or otherwise relinquish control of your mind. If you fall asleep while meditating, and you have followed the procedures we are presenting, you may receive a deep healing that might not be possible if your conscious mind were active. Know that, asleep or awake, you will only receive what you have given your explicit and conscious permission to receive. That's just the way it works.

Finding the Right Space

You will give yourself the best chance for success if you meditate in a quiet place where you will not be interrupted. Designate a place in your home where you will not be distracted by other people, the TV, or the telephone. We recommend you take your phone off the hook or turn on your answering machine to receive any calls.

You will be more comfortable if there are no lights shining in your eyes. Many people find they prefer to turn the lights down or to light some candles. You may think of these preparations as getting yourself "in the mood."

As far as music is concerned, listen to whatever you wish to calm and center your mind before you begin your meditation. But we suggest you turn it off when you actually begin, as the music may hinder your ability to hear your guidance.

We recommend you sit up instead of lying down. If you lie down, it is easy to fall asleep. Sit so that your back is straight and both feet rest on the floor. You may fidget at first, but this will diminish as you become more accustomed to the process of focusing inward.

Finding the Right Time

The best results are obtained when you meditate on a regular schedule. We suggest you start with one session a day — around fifteen minutes is a good starting length. Then, when you can, add a second meditation period and begin to extend the times as you feel ready to do so.

If you can, meditate at the same times every day. Your mind and your body will then *expect* to meditate at these times, and you will be able to move into a meditative state more quickly.

Meditation does not have to be a solitary endeavor. A small group of two or more can often increase your awareness of the energies and will heighten the inner experience of each person. A group can also facilitate getting into a quieter frame of mind in the beginning of a session and provide an opportunity to share experiences afterward.

Breathing

The Masters recommend you concentrate on your breathing while you meditate. We do not recommend you use any extreme breathing techniques you may have learned elsewhere. Simply start by slowly taking one or two deep breaths. Breathe in through your nose and out through your mouth. Breathe in all the way by letting your abdomen expand, filling your lungs completely. Breathe out by letting the air whoosh out. Don't be afraid of making a noise doing this: if you are alone no one will hear you; if you are in a group, everyone else will be doing the same thing!

As you continue to breathe, feel the air enter through your nose and come down into your chest. Feel your chest and abdomen expand and then contract as you exhale. If you feel your mind wandering during the exercises, bring your attention back to your breath.

If you wish, you may follow an additional breathing procedure once or twice during your session: Inhale fully to a slow count of four; hold your breath for another count of four; exhale for a count of four; and pause for a final count of four before inhaling again. Breathe in this manner for a total of three inhalations, then resume your normal breathing. This deep breathing works wonders for quieting your mind and stilling your body. If you do this once at the beginning of your meditation and perhaps once more during it, your mind will begin to associate this method of breathing with meditation, allowing you to reach a meditative state more quickly.

Making your Earth Connection

Imagine yourself creating a connection with the Earth. This can be done by dropping a silver cord of energy from the base of your spine down into the Earth. You can also visualize a rope, an anchor, or the tap root of a tree reaching into the Earth — whatever feels most natural for you. Each person will develop their own most effective grounding image, so feel free to be creative in exploring what works best for you. Your physical body will feel safe when you make this grounding a part of your meditation process and, because the Earth is a living being, she appreciates this acknowledgment from you. She will actually respond to your attention and love. Ask anyone who grows flowers if this is not true.

Affirmations

Affirmations spoken at the beginning of a meditation will help to clarify your intention. It is during meditation that your subconscious mind is most open and receptive to instructions from you. Since the subconscious mind can only understand positive instructions, affirmations should always state what you desire to be, never what you don't want to be.

Affirmations can be a powerful influence on your life, but particularly when used as a part of meditation. They should always be given in the present tense and should be uplifting to you and about you.

Here are some suggested affirmations:

"I am one with my God."

"I am Light and Love."

"I am peace."

"I am one with my Higher Self."

"I am receiving wisdom and understanding."

Feel free to change these affirmations or create new ones for yourself. The affirmation should feel right to you and should represent the way you would *like* to be right now.

Protective Light

There is a very strong protective shield which each of us can invoke that is a form of spiritual energy. We call this the White Light. Your visualized White Light draws some of God's energy into the third dimension. It is pure, healing and enlivening.

The White Light is available to you at any time and can be used in your daily life for protection. For example, we always surround our car and all the people in it with protective White Light before a trip; we visualize our house and children surrounded with it at all times. You can teach your children how to do this for themselves, and it will help them to feel secure in adverse situations.

Spiritual beings in the fifth dimension exist at a more intense level of this Light than we do: this is one of the differentiating features between the third and fifth dimensions. If you visualize this Light in your mind, you will naturally isolate and protect yourself from all lesser influences in any dimension, which cannot tolerate or penetrate it. This Light can become your own personal source of strength. It is universal and can shine anywhere. It is your connection to the Source, which is why it can provide you with such powerful protection. When you make the decision to be connected to the Light, it brings you a whole new set of possibilities and new ideas which were not present in the darkness. Remember, darkness is not a force in itself. It is simply the absence of Light.

Accessing the power and protection of the Light is always but one step away. You simply state the intention that it be established and it is done. You can say something like, *"The Divine White Light comes to me and through me. It completely surrounds me with a shield of protection. It fills my body with peacefulness and serenity. I am strengthened and protected by the White Light."*

We have used this technique of affirming and requesting protection for a long time and strongly recommend that you invoke the protection of the Light at the beginning of each meditation.

Being Empty

One purpose of meditation is to create an absolutely safe place within, a place where you can be at peace and at rest.

Your quiet, inner place can be breached by no one and no thing, unless you allow it.

But it is quite habitual for our rational minds to talk to us about all kinds of things, and it is often difficult to stop this chatter. If someone tells you not to think about elephants, you probably will experience just the opposite: thoughts about elephants will fill your mind. If someone tells you to cease all thoughts, to let your mind be still, most of us can do this for a moment or so. Then all kinds of thoughts begin to well up in our mind, and we jump from one thought to another. Songs or jingles we have heard are particularly pernicious. Sometimes it seems the only way we can get a melody out of our heads is to think about a different one!

In doing these exercises, you will become quiet but you will also allow your mind to fully participate. The exercises use a technique of guided visualization which replaces your random thoughts with specific ones that guide your mind in a desired direction. These specific thoughts actually make the exercises easier and produce better results, because the requirement to "still your mind" or to "cease thinking" is achieved indirectly.

This gentle releasing of your conscious thoughts creates an opening or an emptiness, which will allow your deeper or subconscious thoughts to emerge. Being "empty" is having your conscious mind quiet enough to let new feelings and thoughts enter, unbidden, that pertain to your purpose. In this case, you will be allowing an opening for knowledge about yourself and about God's Love and Light.

We will be asking you to simply concentrate on your breathing, because this has the natural effect of stilling your mind. Breath is life. As you focus on your breath, you will feel more alive. By this process, you are brought back to your own center and the distractions from the outer world (which are not an inherent part of you) fall away. These distractions are what keep us from tuning in to our inner voice and our guidance.

Ending Your Meditation

When you are ready to end your meditation, bring your attention back to your body and your breathing. Take a deep breath or two and, when you are ready, open your eyes.

You may wish to move around a bit: rub your face, shake your hands, or wiggle your toes. If you are sitting and your head feels full, you may wish to bend over and let your head fall between your knees to let any excess energies flow out. Drinking water at the end of a meditation session can also be helpful.

Finally, there is one last step we strongly recommend:

Recording What Happened

End your meditation session by recording what happened. Don't wait until later in the day or the next day to do this. When you are meditating, you are not in a normal waking state of consciousness. Days or weeks later, when you read or listen to what happened, you will naturally have forgotten some of it. Your conscious mind may not believe or remember what happened during your meditations.

Your impressions and feelings are very important, as the meditative state is not as verbal nor intellectual as the waking state. When you later reread what you wrote, you may be surprised at the meaning of the words you chose. Another effect is that you will be forging a link between your inner Higher Self and your outer conscious self.

If you don't record what happened, you may find yourself disappointed because your results and your new insights ended up being far more important than you had anticipated. It's much better to have a recording you don't need and can discard than to wish you had a recording you didn't make!

Make your recording process as easy for yourself as possible. Do what is most natural and comfortable for you. Some people prefer to write longhand in a special notebook or diary reserved for this purpose. We have found a small pocket tape recorder works best for us, and some type of tape recorder is really mandatory for later work when you will be speaking during your meditations. If you decide to use a tape recorder, get a lavalier microphone you can hang around your neck or clip onto your shirt or blouse. This way, you don't have to concern yourself with holding the microphone or speaking at the right volume. You can also get an external AC adaptor. It is very disappointing to have relied on your tape recorder for an important meditation, only to find afterwards that the batteries were ineffective and you lost the entire session.

Let's Get Started

The first three exercises can be used as the foundation and the beginning parts of your meditations. They are designed to help focus and relax your mind, to help you become centered and receptive. Spend several minutes on these centering and relaxing exercises each time you sit down to meditate. They may sound simple to your conscious mind but, if you will take the time to go into meditation and practice them, they can be very powerful and beneficial to you.

As you proceed with the meditation exercises, focus your thoughts on a single object, word, or idea. This will help to screen out the random chatter of your mind as you move into a meditative state. For example, think about the flickering flame of a candle, or a small golden dot of light. Now, in your imagination, bring this image into your body and visualize it resting somewhere near the center of your head, just above the back of your throat. Then, when you are fully relaxed and in a centered and meditative state, you can allow free flowing thoughts to begin. If you find the thoughts of the day intruding, just re-focus your attention on the image you chose until the thoughts fall away again.

Going Within

✧ Be seated in a comfortable position: back straight, feet on the floor, hands resting in an open and receptive position in your lap.

✧ Close your eyes and become conscious of your breathing. As you listen to your breath, you become closer and closer to your center.

✧ Beginning with your feet and lower legs, briefly tighten your muscles, then allow them to relax completely. Inhale as you tighten; exhale as you relax.

✧ Work your way up your body to your thighs, then your lower back and abdomen, chest and shoulders, arms and hands, neck, and finally your facial muscles. Tighten each area as you inhale, then relax it completely as you exhale. Inhale (tighten). Exhale (relax). When you are done, bring your attention back to your breath, feeling completely relaxed.

✧ Become conscious of the Earth beneath your feet. Visualize a connection between yourself and the Earth. You can visualize

{continued}

this anchoring to the Earth in whatever way feels comfortable and works best for you. Whatever image comes to mind ... allow that anchor to connect you to Earth.

✧ Feel your self, your feet, merging with energies of the Earth. Allow that connection to be strong.

✧ Now, make a connection between your self and your Creator. Allow this to be established with a silver cord extending from the top of your head.

✧ You may wish to repeat in your mind any positive affirmation that you desire. For example: "I am one with the Light."

✧ As you sit in this space, connected to Earth and connected to Spirit, think about the gently flickering flame of a candle, or of a small golden dot of light. Bring the image of this light into the center of your head and visualize it resting in a place above the back of your throat.

✧ You are feeling very much at peace. Now, in your mind's eye, imagine a place where you know you will always feel this safe and this protected. It is a place of peace and tranquility, a place where you can go in your quiet meditations. In your imagination, you will be able to visit this special place — your sanctuary, your own temple of Light — during your meditations.

✧ Your sanctuary may be as simple as a private spot on the beach where you can watch the gentle rolling of the ocean, or it may be as elaborate as you wish: a castle, a high tower, or a mountain chalet where you can watch the eagles glide and turn in the air. Your sanctuary is surrounded by and filled with protective White Light.

✧ Spend some time getting familiar with your sanctuary:
What is that under your feet? What is over your head? What is around you? Smell the air. Is there a fragrance here?

✧ Ask your Higher Self to be present and to bring you protection and guidance.   {continued}

✧ Spend as much time as you desire, in silence, enjoying the beauty of this special place. You will be able to return at any time you desire.

✧ Remain open to receive any messages or images which come to you.

✧ When you are ready, bring your attention back to your body and to your breathing. Feeling centered, you return your consciousness back to the room where you are sitting.

Now, take the time to write down what you experienced.

You Succeeded!

There is no way to fail with this exercise. Especially in meditation, your intention is what's important. Often the most significant thing which occurs in meditation is a calming and centering of your mind. Because today's lifestyles are so fast-paced and stressful, this is reward enough in itself. The more you practice, the more apparent will be the results. So, don't be discouraged if you *think* nothing happened.

There is much assistance available to you from the etheric realms. And, if your intention is to gain some knowledge from these exercises, you will be assisted in unexpected ways. You may find yourself alone for half an hour, giving you the quiet time you desire. You may find someone else who is interested in doing the exercises with you, and your joint venture will produce wonderful results.

Be aware that your conscious mind will try to censor what you actually experience with its ideas about what it thinks you *should* or *did* experience. The best way to avoid this is to go with your first impressions, however radical or unexpected they might seem at the time. You may wish to dwell on your first impressions, allowing your mind to follow them. It can be something like walking down a new and unknown path where each step takes you farther on your journey. Once you are centered, don't try to control your thoughts. Just sit quietly and experience what comes, allowing your thoughts to flow freely.

Most of all, do not judge yourself. Although it may look or feel like you're not doing anything, the time spent in meditation is important. You are growing tremendously fast. It is when you are in a meditative state that Spirit can help you and work with you. Spirit comes to you directly when you're meditating. Much of what happens is unspoken, as you work with higher frequencies of energy and new capacities in your brain are being activated.

In your stillness, allow your mind, heart, and throat to be open to these new things you are learning.

Don't be timid or afraid as you are open and sharing the Light.

Be patient and practice, knowing that you cannot fail.

Proceed with these exercises at whatever pace is comfortable for you. Each meditation will begin with a variation of the relaxation exercises. With practice, you will soon find yourself automatically moving into a meditative state, even without consciously going through each of the steps.

The OM

Have you ever seen someone meditating and noticed that they are sitting in a certain way and holding their hands in a particular position? Well, there is actually a purpose for doing this. This is a meditation posture in which you hold your body in a receptive position.

When you turn your hands upward and join your thumb and index finger, you are creating the OM with your hands. The OM is a symbol that is associated with higher consciousness and with God.

The thumb represents God; the index finger represents you — the expanded you which includes your Higher Self. These two forces are symbolically joined and closed in a circle to form the letter "O," representing your union with God. The three remaining fingers, representing the letter "M" and all else, are held symbolically away from the circle.

The OM is also a sound. In addition to holding the OM with your hands, you can sing the sound of the OM with your voice. The OM is a universal sound made as you breathe and allow the joy and peace within your heart to be released as the sounds "O" and "M" (pronounced in a long, gliding transition: OooohMmmm). Practicing the OM will help you to raise your vibration and your consciousness, making you more receptive to higher guidance. When this sound is sung in a group, powerful energies for peace, unity, and love are created by the harmonious blending of voices and spirits. The sound of the OM can be sent as a blessing to the Earth.

The OM can be included as a part of any of your meditations. If the sounding of the OM is a new concept to you, give it a try now.

OM

◇ Sit in a comfortable position, and hold your hands in the OM position. Rest your hands on your lap, palms up, first finger and thumb joined, and the other three fingers pointing away from you.

◇ Close your eyes and focus on your breathing.

{continued}

❖ Move your attention to the back of your throat.

❖ Allow your voice to sing the simple sounds of O then M, lasting the duration of one outbreath.

❖ Repeat this sound several times. If you are in a group, each person will have their own tone and cadence. Together the voices will blend in beautiful harmony.

❖ You (and your group) are now centered, each focused on their own breath, ready to proceed.

How wonderful it is when we can each come to our center and focus inward in this manner. It allows us to detach from the stress in our lives, which may be controlling our actions and affecting our sense of well-being.

Your own personal guides may appear to you in your meditations. They are there to assist you and can provide great wisdom. When the guides appear, they will often give you their names. If you wish to know the name of your special guides, ask them to tell you, loudly and clearly. And then, listen.

Calling Your Guides

❖ Sit in a comfortable position: back straight, feet on the floor, hands resting in a receptive and open position in your lap.

❖ Close your eyes and become conscious of your breathing.

❖ Relax your body, starting with your feet and moving upward to your head.

❖ Affirm your connection to Earth, allowing that connection to become strong.   {*continued*}

✧ Ask for protection. Say to yourself, "I am protected by the golden white Light of the Divine Source."

✧ Visualize this Light surrounding you.

✧ Take yourself to your sanctuary, your special place, and be still within your mind.

✧ Ask that your own personal guides, any Ascended Masters, and your Higher Self join you. These guides represent your own inner wisdom.

✧ If you wish to meet your special guide or guardian angel, state your desire. Allow yourself to be open to whatever comes to you, be it a physical sensation, an emotion, a picture, sounds, or words. You may receive a name as your guide or guardian angel greets you.

✧ You may ask your guide to give you something you need at the moment. It may come as a message or a picture. You may receive a healing, or a release of old emotions that you no longer need.

✧ When you are ready, thank your guide for its presence and assistance.

As you begin meditating, you can ask for guidance from your own inner wisdom. Please do not be discouraged if you ask and you do not immediately sense profound guidance during your meditation. Guidance may not reach your consciousness until later, when an inner knowing arises as a feeling of intuition. That is the answer to your request.

Guidance may also come to you in your dream state. During your dreams you are more open to receive guidance because your conscious mind is fully at rest. In the beginning, especially, you may seem to get more information in your dreams *after* a meditation than during it. But, if you earnestly desire to make these connections, they will eventually come — often in unexpected ways.

If you want to remember your dreams, you can give your subconscious mind an instruction by making an affirmation before going to sleep. Just tell yourself, "I will remember my dreams when I wake up." Then keep a notebook nearby. When you have a dream and it wakes you, be ready to write it down. It will take some discipline to write when you would rather go back to sleep. The dream may seem so pressing and so clear that you are certain you would surely remember it in the morning. But — surprise! It is often gone when you return to your full waking consciousness. Moreover, the words you write will often reveal unexpected meaning, which you will only see as you reread them later — a meaning that you didn't even know existed when you recorded the dream in the middle of the night. We encourage you to be patient and to trust that your unfoldment will occur in its own unique manner, the way most appropriate for you.

⤞ *CHAPTER FOUR* ⤝

Opening to the Light

In our world, we use light to illuminate and to warm. However, the "higher" universes are filled with light of a different quality than we experience here. This light is the actual substance of God's Love. It is also known as Real Light.

If you open yourselves to the light, it is as if you are a tree which has opened its branches to the sunlight. Can you visualize a tree and see how the leaves have spread themselves? The tree arranges its leaves so that they each receive the maximum amount of sunlight throughout the day. It stands tall and straight as it reaches toward the sun. The exercises in this chapter are designed to help you become lighter and thereby more able to experience this Real Light, the Light of God, directly. The exercises will teach you how to receive the most benefit from this energy source, just as a tree knows how to turn its leaves to capture the most light from the sun.

The lighter you can become, the more you will be able to recognize your own Higher Self emerging. The more integrated your conscious self and your Higher Self become, the more able they will be to join into a single consciousness. This is the goal.

Real Light

Real Light is universal. It exists in a dimension we do not ordinarily perceive. This dimension of light is separate, yet it interpenetrates our own.

Real Light can shine anywhere and all creatures have the ability to invite this light to be present in them, giving rise to the traditional idea that God (manifesting as Real Light) exists in every stone, blade of grass, and person on Earth. But when the Light is not invited, either through lack of understanding or through the apparent severing of contact with Source, dark pockets without the Light are created. When large numbers of people have these dark pockets, ideas and beliefs are constructed that do not embrace the Light, because there is no possibility that the Light can be understood.

In the English language, the word "light" has both the meaning "lack of darkness" and "lack of heaviness." The quality that is lacking in darkness is love. In darkness, thoughts and deeds are commited without regard for the consequences. There is no compassion or understanding, which are inherent qualities of the Light.

We can also contrast lightness with heaviness. When people become weighed down with physical and emotional burdens, when they sink into the rut of repetitive existence and boredom, they lose the anticipation and sparkle of life, which is joy. This condition of heaviness has dominated human consciousness as we have forgotten how to allow our own inner Light to shine.

In spite of this, there is always some Light within every being, and there is always the possibility of becoming consciously reconnected to the Source by increasing the amount of Light within. This process of *inner illumination* is happening to a larger number of people now than at any time in the past and is quickening the unfolding of spiritual awakening.

The Light is alive. Its existence is a demonstration of our connection to God in a very real way. The Grace which has been given to us at this time is that we may partake of our earthly dimension along with the dimension of Light, as we become more God-like and grow more fully into our unlimited, greater Selves.

Being Light

Everyone has probably experienced the emotional states of being "light-hearted" and "heavy-hearted." "Heavy" or "negative" emotions (such as fear, anxiety, anger, guilt, and self-reproach) must be suspended, at least temporarily. You are attempting to approach the highest parts of your self and these emotions will keep you locked into your ego-self, and away from your goal. When you put aside negative emotions and unloving thoughts, and replace them with openness and trust, your ego-self can align with its higher counterpart.

As the Light comes into this dimension and into each person, the possibilities for embracing it or rejecting it become more frequent. When you choose to receive the Light, it will bring a whole new set of possibilities and ideas to you that were simply not present in the darkness. As this happens, you will become more whole. You will become aware of aspects of your Self which were hidden or not available before and you will sense your own lightness expanding more and more. As you acknowledge your connection to the Light, you will naturally be stepping onto the path your Higher Self wishes for you. Although some Light has always reached you, once you make this acknowledgement, you will begin to experience more of this Light.

Just as embracing the Light provides impetus by propelling you along your divine path, rejecting the Light creates a recoil or ricochet effect. When someone experiences the Light but then rejects it, they will go careening off in another direction faster than they would have if they had never encountered the Light.

The quantity of Real Light available is increasing now, because the veil that has insulated us from this Light is thinning and more Light is getting through to us. Personal activities and emotions have more velocity. People are either being propelled toward the Light or away from it with greater speed than they have ever been in the past. This new intensity is like turning up the voltage, or pressing down on the accelerator. Choices come into focus with sharper contrast, so there is less ambiguity and confusion, and the consequences of those choices become apparent much more quickly.

There are vast quantities of this Real Light available to us from an unlimited source. This increased Light is going to provide the catalyst for change. It is the foundation upon which higher dimensions can be understood and upon which reality can be changed, reshaped, and re-energized.

Light is love and Light is joy. As you practice unconditional love and unconditional joy, you will bring about a clearer awareness of the Light, thereby strengthening your own body of light. As this happens, the many facets of your Higher Self begin to merge, the veils of illusion begin to dissolve, and you begin your ascension back into the dimension of undiluted Real Light, where you were always meant to be.

As human beings, our bodies are the vessels for this Divine Light, which is being infused from the Creator. They are capable of receiving and holding vast quantities of Light and can now sustain greater concentrations of it. Therefore, as we become lighter, we manifest new capabilities for ourselves which didn't exist prior to this infusion.

The Light can only be fully present in a vessel which is whole — without breaks and flaws, or rough and hardened spots in it. As you work with your own inner guidance, the exercises in this book will help you become a whole vessel for Light, without obstructions and blocks which prevent it from flowing to you and through you. The exercises are designed to help you release the pain and blocks which have been created by past experiences, leaving you with the knowledge and wisdom you have gained.

Your vessel should be opened wide at the top, so that a golden ray of Light can be allowed to enter freely. Light-heartedness is one of those qualities which will help you to turn yourself into a Light vessel; laughter is one approach to light-heartedness. For when you are laughing, you release tension, you are open, and your vibrational rate is naturally accelerated. The next exercise is designed to give you the experience of lightening yourself through laughter.

Light and Laughter

✧ Start by relaxing and centering yourself.

✧ Sit with your feet flat on the floor and be aware of your connection to the Earth.

✧ Move the focus of your concentration slowly up your body. Be aware of any tension, releasing it as you move your attention to the top of your head, your crown chakra.

{*continued*}

✧ Focus on your breathing and ask Sananda, Kuthumi or any other guides to be with you.

✧ Visualize a shaft of light, streaming down to you from above and see yourself standing tall and straight like a sturdy tree. Every leaf — your every desire, emotion, and thought — is exposed to the light. As the day progresses and the sun moves across the sky, no leaf is completely hidden.

✧ Feel the radiance of the sun shining down on you. This is the way that we can easily be touched by the warmth of the Divine Light. We know that it is there, that it is waiting for us to simply stop and let it touch us.

✧ Feel the Light which is coming down to you run through your body and into the Earth. Be aware of the sense of warmth and connection you feel.

✧ Now laugh out loud: "Ha, ha, ha!" Make it a joyful belly laugh. If you feel silly, so much the better! Honor yourself by smiling at your courage to laugh all by yourself, alone, with your eyes closed.

✧ See if your smile doesn't last awhile, as you contemplate your ridiculousness. If you lose it, just repeat, "Ha, ha, ha!" again.

✧ Remember to concentrate on your breath. Repeat the affirmation "I am laughter and I am Light" to yourself.

✧ Now surround yourself with a silver-white light. Let it come down from above your head and surround you. Let it permeate you from head to toe.

✧ Continue this exercise for a few minutes. Allow yourself to bask in the lightness and joy you are now feeling.

✧ When you are ready, bring your attention back to the room in which you are sitting.

———⟫⊙⟪———

If you feel ready for more, you may proceed to the next exercise. If you wish to stop for now, we recommend you repeat this last exercise just prior to beginning the next one. But above all, do this exercise often. It is a wonderful tonic and preparation for becoming a Light Being.

Perhaps the most astonishing result of opening to the Light has to do with that other aspect of Light, lack of heaviness. Your mind can literally float into higher dimensions when you become light enough. A significant part of you will be so light, it will automatically be attracted to the Universal Light. And as you practice being light, you will become a shining light, a Light Being. The energy vibrations of your body will actually begin to be raised, which will bring you more fully into the fifth dimension.

Lightness and Floating

✧ Be seated in a comfortable and receptive position: back straight, feet on the floor, hands resting palms up in your lap.

✧ Close your eyes and concentrate on your breathing as you relax your body.

✧ As you take in each breath, allow joy to fill your body. Breathe in the joy of the day, the joy of who you are growing into being.

✧ As you expand your lungs with your breath, allow yourself to imagine your expanded magnificence, which extends beyond your physical body.

✧ Affirm your connection to Earth and ask for protection. Say aloud, "I am protected by the White Light of the Divine Source."

{continued}

✧ You are practicing what it would feel like if you could float. Allow your arms to become lighter and lift them slowly, letting them move back and forth if you desire. You may repeat to yourself, "I am floating in the Light."

✧ Be aware of the subtle energy you are beginning to feel. Allow your head to gently roll or move as it desires. You may want to move it back and forth or rock it from side to side. Just allow yourself to easily move with the energy.

✧ Now, in your mind, float into the air. Just imagine that you are floating over your chair. You may see yourself stretched out on your back, as if you were floating down a lazy river on a comfortable air mattress, drifting gently in the current. If you feel daring (and why not? — you are just imagining!) you may roll over, stretch your arms out to your sides or in front of you, and fly around. Try loop-the-loops, barrel rolls, dives and climbs — anything you can imagine. In your mind, you do not move around by flapping your arms, or kicking your feet. A thought can create motion.

✧ Now imagine a snow-white cloud above you. Fly into it. It's not a real cloud of water droplets; it's a cloud of brilliant light. It's as warm and soothing as being in a swimming pool filled with water of exactly the right temperature.

✧ Now laugh aloud, "Ha, ha, ha!" Let yourself smile and feel the joy of laughter.

✧ Just float and enjoy. Be aware of what you are experiencing.

✧ When you are ready, float back down to your chair. Know that you are sitting in your chair, but you have brought some of the Light back with you.

✧ Now, open your eyes and be present again in the room in which you are sitting.

In all of your meditation sessions, we suggest you affirm your clear and strong connection to your own Higher Self. When you go within to connect with your own wisdom, you will be connecting with your Higher Self, that part of yourself which is all-knowing and can provide the guidance and direction you are seeking. The next exercise is designed to help you make this connection with your Higher Self.

Contacting Your Higher Self

◇ Start by relaxing and centering yourself, feet flat on the floor.

◇ Be aware of your connection to the Earth.

◇ Move your attention slowly up your body. Be aware of any tension, releasing it as you focus on the top of your head or crown chakra.

◇ Visualize a shaft of light streaming down to you from above.

◇ Affirm your connection to your Higher Self. Visualize yourself bringing this connection down, right through the top of your head, until the energy fills your body. Sense the oneness you now feel with your Higher Self, the wisest and most loving part of you.

◇ You may ask questions you would like your Higher Self to answer. Then open yourself to receive the information. The answers to your questions may come in the form of words, pictures, sensations, or feelings. Take your first impressions as the answer. If you feel a hunch that a certain answer has been given, act as if this is the answer.

◇ Perhaps you don't feel that an answer was given at this time. Allow that to be. The answer you are seeking may occur to you within the next few days as an inner knowing that something is

{*continued*}

right or wrong or it may reveal itself to you as an increase in your enthusiasm.

◇ Notice how you feel during this meditation. Is there a certain sensation in some part of your body (perhaps a smile, or perhaps you just feel comforted)? This is your Higher Self communicating with you in your physical body. Remember this feeling, for when you feel it in the future, you will know your Higher Self is nearby.

◇ Take as long as you like, and enjoy the experience of a wonderful communion.

◇ When you are ready, you may give your thanks and bring your attention back to the room.

Part of the beauty of going within is coming to know more about the hidden aspects of yourself. You will be able to get in touch with your own true essence and discover an inner beauty or a sense of purpose you hadn't felt before. The exercise of "The Rose" is designed to do just this. If you can, find a friend or a group and do this beautiful exercise of discovery together.

Your Rose

◇ Start by relaxing and centering yourself. Sit with your feet flat on the floor and be aware of your connection to the Earth. Know that the Earth supports you and strengthens you. Just as the plants do, you can draw upon the Earth for strength.

{*continued*}

❖ Move the focus of your concentration slowly up your body. Be aware of any tension, releasing it as you move your attention to the top of your head, your crown chakra.

❖ Focus on your breathing and ask your Higher Self and guides to be with you.

❖ Affirm that you are surrounded and protected by the White Light from the Divine Source and visualize a shaft of White Light streaming down to you from above.

❖ Now see a beautiful flower resting at the top of your head. This may be a rose, a lotus blossom, or any other flower. See its petals opening to the light from above. Feel your flower absorbing this light of pure love.

❖ Imagine that you are this flower, receiving light from above, carrying it through the stem of your body, and running it straight into the Earth.

❖ Now, imagine that you can hold this flower (which represents your Self) out in front of you. Take it in your hands and see it in all of its beauty, its blossom opened to the light. Notice the color and texture of the petals. Smell its fragrance.

❖ As you look at this flower more closely, notice that there is something hidden in the very center. This is your special gift. It may be a message, it may be a picture. It may be something about yourself that you have never seen before. Again, allow the images or thoughts to come, and go with your first impressions.

❖ Take a moment to focus your attention on this new awareness you have just received. Then, when you are ready, return your consciousness to the room where you are sitting and give thanks for your new understanding.

Releasing Fears

In the higher dimensions, beings live without fear. They see their paths of service more clearly and spend much time discovering how they can best fulfill their goals. They are fully aware of God's love supporting them at all times, and it is "natural" to trust in the "Divine Plan" for their lives.

On Earth, however, there are many things that we do not understand or cannot "see," and fears often rise up about them. Know that your Higher Self has no experience of fear. Fear only arises when you think about things that have frightened you in the past, or that you worry may come to pass in the future.

Fright is one thing. It occurs when there is real danger and then is over. Fear is different: it can persist long after the fright is gone. Fear is the single most significant barrier to personal growth because it keeps you from moving forward and from embracing changes. It is possible to create the experiences of your life so that when you meet something new and unknown, you will be able to meet it without fear. A situation may be unfamiliar, but you will not be paralyzed by the emotion of fear.

Those who do not understand the concept of establishing protection for themselves may often find much cause for alarm. They fear the things around them that they do not know about. In fact, they even fear the things that are not around them at all — things they have heard about in distant places, where the danger to them is actually very small or nonexistent. When you think about all the things that *could* happen, you can actually create experiences in your life which are contrary to your desires. Your fears can actually attract those things to you. This happens because you attract those things to which you give your attention. The focus of your attention becomes your unconscious intention. This works for fear as well as it works for love or prosperity.

This exercise on "Releasing Fear" is designed to help you let go of your perceived limitations, some of which manifest as fears. Perhaps it is the fear of failure, the fear of change, the fear that you are not up to doing something you strongly desire, or the fear that you will not be provided for monetarily in the times to come. As you are going through the exercise, whatever comes into your mind is what you are ready to release. So we encourage you to take a deep breath as you prepare to release those fears which are limiting you.

This exercise will illustrate one of the important ways Archangel Michael can serve you. You will ask him to use his powerful blue sword of Light to cut the psychic cords that bind you to your fears. You can ask Michael to release you from your fears, to help you find the courage and the power to do those things in life which you most strongly desire — those things which are in alignment with your nature and your purpose here on Earth.

 Releasing Fear

✧ Be seated in a comfortable position.

✧ Close your eyes and become conscious of your breathing.

✧ Relax your body and allow any tension within it to gently fade away.

✧ Affirm your connection to Earth and ask for protection. Say to yourself, "I am completely surrounded and protected by the White Light of the Divine Source."

{continued}

✧ In your mind, take yourself to your special place (that sacred sanctuary where you know you are safe), and allow your mind to be still.

✧ Call upon your special guides, your Higher Self, the Ascended Masters, and your guardian angels to watch over and protect you.

✧ See the White Light surround you. Ask Archangel Michael to place a field of protection around your home so that no negative influences can get through to you.

✧ When you reach a state of relative quiet, ask Archangel Michael, with his powerful and swift sword of Light, to join you.

✧ Allow any fears which are ready to be released to gently come into your awareness. You only need to be aware of the fears; you do not need to experience them.

✧ Then, see these fears gathered into a ball and surrounded by White Light. Know that they are separate from you.

✧ The space you have created is absolutely safe and sacred. You are bathed in crystalline White Light. You are aware of your guardian angels, who constantly watch over you and attempt to smooth your path.

✧ You are aware that your Higher Self is firmly and constantly connected to you through a silver cord which comes in through the top of your head, goes down through each energy center in your body, and all the way down into the Earth.

✧ Ask Archangel Michael to use his sword of blue light to cut the cords that bind you to any and all fears that you wish to leave behind. Whatever they are, know that you only need state your request, and it is done instantly.

✧ Sit in quietness and meditation as you experience being surrounded by beautiful healing energy.

{*continued*}

✧ You may ask questions, ask for additional healings, or end the exercise. Wait for any additional messages or impressions. Then, when you feel completed with this session, you may give your thanks and return your consciousness back to the room.

You may adapt or extend this releasing exercise as you see fit. You may ask to be released from perceived limitations. You may ask to be released from any relationships or situations which are not for your highest good and know that releasing on the inner level precedes release on the outer level, in your waking life. Try this exercise a few times and see what happens for you.

In ascension work, the Masters ask us to release our attachments to material things. This doesn't mean we have to give up all the things in our life, but it does mean we shouldn't remain emotionally attached to them. Indeed, you may find, after asking Michael to release you from your attachments, that you still enjoy your comforts, good food, and good friends, but you are less attached to the idea of "having to have" them. Perhaps this is just because your desires are shifting to a different set of priorities, and certain physical objects and material possessions are becoming less important.

As we move forward into the new age on our planet, we must become more integrated with our true natures. Our vibrations will actually be increasing as the spiritual parts of ourselves become awakened. This process (ascension) will require us to release those fears and self limitations which have been binding us to this density. Fears have created a consciousness burden — a heaviness — and must be released before we can begin living our lives in the fullness and Light which it is our destiny to reclaim.

⇥ CHAPTER FIVE ⇤

Channeling

There has been a cosmic shield around the Earth for thousands of years. This shield has led man to believe that he is alone in the universe, that life beyond planet Earth is at least questionable and certainly a mystery. Our perception of reality has been limited by what we can sense with our third-dimensional senses of hearing, smelling, seeing, touching, and tasting. Anything beyond that has conjured up disbelief and skepticism. Now, this shield — the veil over our eyes — is being lifted. We are regaining our ability to receive and interpret forms of communication that are new to us.

Our world has changed in the last few years, largely because of these influences we cannot see. You may realize that you are changing as well. Desires are manifesting themselves more quickly than ever; time seems to have been accelerated, and miracles are becoming more commonplace. Are you aware of them?

Now there is new information available which is being showered down from the heavens. All that we need to do is learn how to *receive* it. Mankind will actually be developing new senses as we and the planet move forward into the new age. One of the new skills which will become more prevalent is a method of receiving telepathic information, often called "channeling."

Channeling is a method for being more receptive, and listening with expanded awareness. Channeling is one of the ways God communicates with us, and He withholds it from no one. It is an innate capability in each of us which can be discovered and developed with practice.

Your discovery of channeling may start with intuition, compelling feelings, dreams, or messages which seem to pop into your head. Since we all have the potential built into our brains for telepathic communications, most of us have had some experience of these things already.

As you open your channels of communication, a link is established and you will begin to bridge the gap between dimensions. In fact, you may think of **bridging** as another word for the channeling process.

There are basically two kinds of channeling. Conscious channeling is where the channel (you) remains fully conscious, aware of the proceedings, and in control. In the second form of channeling (trance channeling), the channel is in a trance or an altered state of consciousness and will probably not remember what was said during the communication. We only teach techniques for **conscious channeling**.

In conscious channeling, you will not be giving up control or be taken over by another entity, in any way. You will be creating a communications bridge, listening to and translating or relaying the messages you have received. These messages may seem to you like thoughts; you may hear a voice, or you may see a picture. As a channel you can then write or speak the message you have received, in order to record it.

One way to think of yourself is as a tremendous satellite dish. In fact, the human brain and the entire human body are full of receptors which can receive telepathic messages, guidance, and illumination from the heavens. If this mechanism were turned off, it would not receive any signals even though they would continue to exist. As we start the process of connecting with our guidance and bridging the communications gap, we are making the conscious decision to put our antenna up and to listen. You are the one who will determine the nature of the channeled messages you will listen to, just as you can determine what channel you are going to watch when you turn on your television set.

Discernment

The information you receive always comes through the filter of your Higher Self. As you begin to channel, you can trust that you have great personal strength and assistance. However, it is wise to ask for protection by calling upon your Higher Self and any other Masters whom you choose. We like to set up loving protection by surrounding ourselves and our house with the golden-white Light of the Divine Source. This is a way of acknowledging that we are a part of something greater and a way of asking God to come to us through whatever guides he chooses. It is a way of being thankful.

When you invoke the protective Light, it is a way of being respectful and a way of being in alignment with your Higher Self and your Creator. You can call upon anyone else you desire to be with you: Sananda (or Jesus), Mother Mary, Buddha, God, your guardian angels. You remain in control as you ask for the support which best fits into your belief system. If you visualize this light in your mind, you will naturally be protected from all lesser influences which cannot tolerate it. Visualizing the protective White Light about you is a fail-safe procedure for contacting only the highest beings.

As you call upon the Light, you will be bringing God's energy to surround and fill you. It is pure, healing, and enlivening. It can give you protection and, as you reaffirm your connection to the Light, you will actually be attracting your Light Body to yourself. You will be coming more into alignment with it and you will actually be bringing forth more of the Light from within yourself. The Law of Attraction is at work here. When you put yourself in a positive, light state of being, you will be attracting to yourself other things which are light and positive. The more you bring the Light in around you, the more this begins to happen, and the more you build your bridge into Light.

You may wish to add additional affirmations to your meditations when you are going to be channeling. You will naturally develop your own affirmations and invocations, but the following examples will help you get started:

"I am the living Light."

"I am one with the Divine Source and united with my Higher Self."

"I gain strength from this union, and I realize my fullest potential."

"I sense fulfillment in all that I do."

"I am guided and protected by a radiant, golden white Light which emanates from the highest source. This Light surrounds me and uplifts me."

"All members of my household are protected by this Light."

"I am granted complete invisibility from all negative forces."

"I call upon the angels, archangels, and Ascended Masters to be with me and to assist me with their guidance."

There are some universal laws surrounding channeling which must be upheld by all beings. The primary one is that each of us is sovereign in our own space! You do not ever need to give your control away. We each have absolute free will. This comes from our Higher Self and makes it impossible for us to be coerced. It is our free will which determines what we are and what we will become. The Masters (the ascended beings) and the angels will not ever breach your personal power.

Any being that seems to come to you in your meditations or channelings can be judged with only one criterion: Does that being want something *from* you, or does it only want something *for* you? There is no need to give away any power to another being. The Ascended Masters want nothing from our plane of existence. In fact, the Ascended Masters ardently wish for us to take back and **use** all of our powers. You will know their presence because it will feel full of love and protection. When you are channeling an ascended being, you may find yourself smiling or feel your heart expand with love. What you experience and receive in your channelings will assist you in your own ascension.

Assistance from the Masters

The Masters in this book present themselves factually; there are no "thees" or "thous," and there is no historical religious dogma. Often they are humorous. They are understandable and always on the mark. Because they exist in a realm of timelessness and love, they can be of great assistance to us, and that, indeed, is what they desire.

Kuthumi is an Ascended Master who assisted us when we began to channel. He had the following message for us about channeling:

I am here to give you some assistance on being open to the Light, on creating a channel. A channel of water, you know, is opened up and allows the water to move easily and clearly from one place to another. A channel of communication is a bridge. The channel that you are keeping open to the heavens is important at this time, so that each one would receive his own personal guidance without having to depend upon the television, the media, or the newscast reports, which all provide information that has been screened and controlled. You cannot allow yourselves to depend fully on this public information. At this time, the only information which you can trust is the information which comes to you through the channel that you have opened — your own private channel of information from the Divine Source.

To keep these channels open, you must trust in your own intuition. Take time to be silent and to go within and to check what is on your own personal viewing screens. The channels are open wide. Guidance and information and support is pouring down to each individual in a shaft of light. Earlier you were visualizing the connections to the Creator, to the Divine Source, as being a thin silver thread, but what is open now for communications is a shaft of light. It is available to every person. It is a shaft of support and strength and personal guidance. This is available if you will only take the time to receive it. You do not need to open the doors — the doors are open. It is a part of our support and our service to you at this time of great turmoil and unrest on your planet.

When you are beginning to channel, there is a tendency to wait until you have a complete thought formulated in your mind before you begin to speak. But Kuthumi advises us that we have to trust and just begin to speak the words as they come to us. It is like being an interpreter. You wait to receive an image or a thought and then relay that along, making way for the next. Avoid the tendency to make your own interpretations as you receive the thoughts or words, and allow them to flow through you as clearly and without obstruction as possible.

This is how Kuthumi explains the channeling process:

On beginning to channel the Ascended Masters, it is important to know that "You don't need to know." When you are channeling, you make yourself an open vessel. If water were flowing from a stream and you were to try to catch it, you would put the vessel or bucket under the falling water. The information which is being poured upon the Earth at this time can be thought of much like the water in this stream, or like water from a falling rain.

New information is being made available now to mankind. It is being poured down from the heavens — a shower of beautiful rain, coming to quench the thirst of a parched and thirsty land. So this is as it will be received, for mankind is so very thirsty. You have struggled for lifetime upon lifetime trying to understand the meaning of life, trying to understand your true natures ... knowing you were created in God's image, but often wondering why. What was the purpose of life? What was the meaning of it? And now, in this new and glorious time of enlightenment, the heavens have opened up and the drops of rain — the silver drops of information and guidance — are showering the Earth. Think of a gentle shower of rain.

You need to be open, to create an opening. The larger the opening of the vessel, the more you can receive of this glorious, soothing information being showered down. So, step number one is to allow yourself to be open, to be a receptacle. As you use the techniques given to you earlier in this book on being open for meditation, you will be open to receive love and guidance from the Ascended Masters.

In the Bible, it is spoken that to receive the Kingdom of Heaven, you must be innocent as children, trusting and eager to learn without judgement. So it is as you are beginning to channel. Information is received and moves through you with your intellect set aside, without judgment. You receive a piece of information — a thought, a picture, or a word. It is impossible to know the end of the story when you begin, because it is coming to you and through you from a higher source. So, as you trust and allow it to flow, it is allowed to continue.

The easiest way to begin is to just say "Hello." If a name pops into your head, speak that name. Become that name. The power of your channeling abilities will become magnified as you do this. Speak, for example, "I am Kuthumi, teacher and bearer of Light." As you trust and speak or write the words, you are creating an opening for the next thought to present itself. It is rather like opening the gates of a dam. The dam may be full, but if a gate is not opened not one drop of water can flow out.

As you receive the thoughts or images, as you allow guidance to flow through you, you will begin to understand your own personal connection to the Divine Source. The greatest information that man can receive at this time is pouring forth from the heavens. It is new information for a new time. It is time to gain your knowledge directly from the Source rather than trusting another's interpretations and information. We are each connected to the Divine Source by a silver thread and connected to each other by this thread as well. When you allow yourselves to receive direct guidance, you are strengthening this connection.

— *Kuthumi*

Getting Started

Like any new skill, channeling requires practice. Kuthumi gave us the "Just Say Hello" exercise which follows. We find that it is very supportive to have two or more people get together to practice these exercises. If you are going to try this exercise in a group, it's a good idea to decide in advance who is going to channel first. The extra pressure of being in the *hot seat* actually seems to intensify the energies and helps you get started. The other people in your group will also be sending you energy as they focus their attention on you when it's your turn. This will give you another little boost.

You may want to have a tape recorder or a notebook handy, especially if you are channeling alone. When you are in the meditative state and thoughts or words occur to you, you will be able to record them. When you look at them later on, it will be evident that they were beyond your *normal* thoughts, even though it may not have seemed so at the time.

When you are channeling, it is valuable to assume the voice of the I AM presence. What that means is, as Kuthumi suggested, when you hear a name, speak the name and own it for the time: *"I am _____ ."* For example, you would say, *"I am Kuthumi."* This will help you come into alignment and to make the shift required to allow the energies and messages to move freely through you. It will help you to match your energies to those of your guide and to move your own intellect aside so that it does not interfere with the message.

If you desire more clarity, you can repeat the affirmation, *"I am a clear and open channel,"* as often as desired throughout the meditation. You can also ask the Masters to *turn up the volume.* They will never give you more energy or more information than you are able to handle.

Know that your guide will leave when the session is over. Sometimes your guide will tell you goodbye. Sometimes you will feel the energies begin to weaken, and you will know that the channeling is over. You will return to your waking state of consciousness — perhaps lightened — but very much the same you!

When you are complete with the session, thank your guide for coming to you and for the guidance or information you have received.

Just Say Hello

To begin, get ready to meditate. Remember the techniques you learned about being receptive in meditation.

✧ Allow yourself to be comfortable and to release the cares and thoughts of the day.

✧ Feel the awareness of your surroundings begin to melt.

✧ Focus your mind on your breath and, as you breathe in, allow your abdomen to expand, bringing the breath in all the way down to your belly. Then exhale, forcing out all of the air, and preparing yourself for fresh new air to enter — cleansing, cool air.

✧ When you have become quiet, begin with some conscious breathing. Breathe in fully and deeply; hold the breath to the count of four, then release the breath and exhale completely: Whoosh. Repeat this breath three times.

> Breathe in   ...1...2...3...4
> Hold breath   ...1...2...3...4
> Breathe out   ...1...2...3...4
> Hold count   ...1...2...3...4

{*continued*}

✧ Continue breathing in fully and breathing out, concentrating on your breath, the breath of life. Now you are more relaxed; tension and tightness have been released from your body. If there is still any tension remaining, you can let it go with your next breath.

✧ If you desire to connect with higher guidance, you may speak the phrases silently to yourself:

"I am one with the Light."
"I am protected by the Light."
"I am the Light and love of the Divine Source."
"I am a clear and open channel."

✧ Imagine a shaft of Light from above, coming down and showering your body with gentle drops of silver light. Bring the energy down, through your crown, through your energy centers, and into the Earth.

✧ Become aware of any sensations of energy in your body, such as tingling or a feeling of lightness. Each Master will have their own special signal, so be aware of any physical sensations which may be occurring.

✧ The way to open the door when you feel this presence is to simply say "Hello," welcoming it. When you do this you may receive a message. There is some surrender and trust required here, as you allow yourself to experience the energies.

✧ A name may come to you. If it does, then speak the name using the voice of the I AM presence. You will say "I am ..." and then speak the name. By doing this, you are becoming "tuned in" to the energies that are coming through.

✧ Speak any words or thoughts as they form. Do not analyze the words, just let them flow. You may choose to speak the words or you may choose to write them, but it is important that you allow them to move through you, for that's what channeling is

{*continued*}

about — becoming a conduit for information. If you hold on to the words, the flow is stopped. So, as you receive the words, allow them to flow through you, making room for more.

✧ When you sense the energies departing (or fading), you will know that the channeling is complete. Your guide may tell you goodbye or may simply fade away. Sever any psychic connections by asking that this be done, and bring your presence back to the room.

Remember to record the messages you receive, either on tape or in writing.

You may have had resounding success on your first attempt, or perhaps the messages were a little foggy and unclear. It is important not to be critical and not to expect too much the first time. You are practicing tuning in to energies that you may not have even known about before reading this book. Your ability to receive information will develop with practice.

When you are first attempting to channel, you may receive a name or a picture and nothing more. You may receive only a sentence or two. That's wonderful! Acknowledge yourself for your efforts and trust that your abilities will develop when the time is right. Don't be discouraged if you feel that nothing happened on your first attempt; remember that you are discovering a new skill, and it will take time and practice to develop proficiency with it.

The Masters who are here to assist you can be more direct with you as these channels of communication become wider. More complete messages will be permitted to flow back and forth between you, especially in *your* direction — from them to you.

In the beginning, it is as if they have to whisper and to speak very slowly. Then, once the channels become more open, they can speak at full strength and at a normal volume and pace for you. After a while, you may begin to notice that the words that you channel are coming through faster, at normal conversational speed. This is ideal. It is a good pace. It matches the amount of information being transmitted with the attention span of your memory and your ability to maintain an open channel. All you have to do is to create the time and the space, and trust that your abilities will develop when the time is right.

How Do You Know It's Real?

It's common to question whether you are really doing it. It's common to wonder if the thoughts aren't actually your own, because that is often what it feels like. At first, you may not be able to tell the difference between "channeling" and "thinking." This is okay, and you shouldn't worry about it.

Channeling, like any other new skill, is developed with practice. In the beginning we only got a few words and then a few sentences. As we learned to trust more completely, and learned to match our energies to those of the Masters, the channelings began to feel more natural. Kuthumi's advice to "let the words and thoughts flow" is the key. Some people see pictures or get images, some hear the words, others just have the words occur to them like their own thoughts. Sometimes you will receive information in a combination of these forms. If you get a picture or vision, attempt to describe it or draw it. Once again, you need to trust your own inner wisdom.

You can generally feel a physical sensation of increased energy in your body before the messages come. That is, you can feel the energetic presence of the being. When you connect with your Higher Self, there is sometimes a tingling sensation, like raindrops of energy falling on your head and skin.

Each of the Ascended Masters may have a special sign for you. It is generally a feeling of energy in a particular part of the body. For example, Sananda may feel like an expansion in the heart area, angels may feel uplifting, Kuan Yin may present a tingling in the hands, and so forth. The signs will be special to you and will not necessarily match the signs a Master uses with anyone else. You can ask for a sign and it will be given. As you continue doing this, you will become familiar with your guides and familiar with their signals to you.

Then, if you can follow Kuthumi's guidance and allow the words to flow, there may be a noticeable difference in the words you have used and in the character of your voice. There may be a change in the inflection of your words. If you have made a tape recording, you may be able to notice this when you play it back. This becomes even more obvious if you channel more than one entity in a session.

It *is* real if it *feels* real, and although it's common to have doubts, they are really unnecessary. Have no expectations and make no judgements about your results. Learning to be open to your own internal guidance is the goal. It is a personal process. Your accomplishments will be personal triumphs; the prize will be expanded knowingness and a new sense of oneness with God.

There is much healing that is required for mankind. Healing includes releasing the pain and the disease carried in the emotional, spiritual, and physical bodies. This is the lifetime in which all psychic burdens can be left behind. In fact, for all who will ascend, this is to be so. It is time now to release your pain, your guilt, and your feelings of limitation, in order to become lighter and to prepare yourself for the new age.

We encourage you to open yourself to the loving assistance which is being offered to us at this time by the Ascended Masters. As stated by Sananda:

I bring healing for the heart. I have been a great teacher on this, your Earth. I taught about strength and, yes, about suffering. My message was of hope.

When you connect with your Divine Father and maintain your focus on the Light, the distractions and problems around you in your material world do not penetrate your soul, because you know you are connected with a higher power. When you are truly one with God, you can maintain an inner peace.

No love on Earth can equal the Love of God which fills your heart and gives you serenity. In your relationships, you try to achieve this wholeness which you can only achieve when you feel a union with the Divine Source. The world is so full of people striving for this outwardly. It must be done internally — inwardly, on a spiritual path.

I, Sananda, am here with you. I am pleased for you to call upon me, and I will work with you. You will find yourself changed.

CHAPTER SIX

Healing

The Healing Process

"Healing" is a term we usually apply to the process our bodies perform after an injury. Although we usually think about healing in terms of the physical body, there is another kind of healing which is instrumental in physical healing. This is emotional healing, and it is a major part of the ascension process.

A synonym for the process of healing is "wholing": it is the process of becoming whole. It is returning to a state of harmony and balance, to the ideal. It is a way of connecting with your strength and re-empowering yourself. Becoming lighter and casting off the burdens of anger, resentment, limitation, and unworthiness is a requirement for returning to our true natures. Recently, there has been a great deal of focus on the process of doing this, because mankind is ready to exist in an expanded state of wholeness and fullness.

When you truly understand that you were created in the image of God and that each person is connected to God and to each other, you can begin to embrace the divinity in every one. With this perspective, you can begin to understand that anger, resentment, and the rest are not worth it anymore, and you can cease to have these emotions. There is a brief moment in any situation when you have the ability to make a choice about your reactions — a moment *before* your emotions get hooked and take control.

The key to reaching this higher perspective lies in knowing that you are much more than you ever suspected — that you are truly divine and connected to the divine. When you know that for yourself, you will know it for all others. It is this perspective which allows you to change your patterns of behavior and see the world with acceptance and love. Sananda tells us:

> *So many people are feeling so much pain, but they don't know why. It's the **not understanding** that makes the pain so intense. You cannot imagine the joy which will be experienced when humanity sighs a sigh and, with one giant breath, leaves its pain behind. Yes, this ascension for mankind is going to happen soon.*
>
> *The pain of man is such a burden! It is not only a burden for people because there is so much pain in the human heart, but — because each person is like a crystal, running energy into the Earth — it is also a tremendous burden upon the Mother, our Earth. The Earth feels the pain of mankind just as you might feel the pain for a loved one.*

And so, at this time there is much assistance available to heal the emotional pain. Sometimes, part of the healing involves re-experiencing old pains as they are being released from the emotional or physical bodies. If you allow the Masters to work with you, this can be but brief. It can pass in a moment. Of course, if you wish to hang on to your pain, that is your choice. But it is the Master's goal to assist you in moving beyond your pain — to lift your burden of pain so that you can become lighter, light enough to ascend.

Now there is help available to everyone who has a desire to move forward in consciousness and to elevate their way of being in the world. You can ask for this help and know that it will be given.

Several months ago, we heard a song in our church which had the refrain "Kiss it Goodbye." The song was about releasing those things in our lives that we no longer desire. In the chorus, we were to take those feelings which we no longer wanted to be a part of us, place them in our hands, and then kiss them goodbye. As we go through the motions of placing something in our hand, kissing it, and then flinging it away, we simply blow away our frustrations. They are gone and they are released — in love — to move freely away.

We have found this to be a light-hearted and effective way to diffuse feelings of anger or frustration. It has been fun for us to use this technique in our relationship, because it is so simple and because it works. It's kind of a secret code for releasing bad feelings, and we always end up laughing as we see how simple and how effective this little action is.

Changing familiar patterns of behavior requires practice. You can use this technique easily no matter where you are, at any time, and as often as you like. If some old feeling creeps in, just blow it away again. Then, pretty soon, it stops coming back because you have interrupted the habit of having it hang around.

Shortly after learning this method of releasing, it was brought to our attention again, during a channeling with a Master known as Hilarion. The topic of releasing was being discussed and he said, "I believe you already have a method for doing this — the 'Kiss-It-Goodbye' strategy." This was a verification for us regarding the value of this technique. The person doing the channeling was someone who knew nothing about the song.

This technique can be done any time, but it is most powerful if you do it while meditating. You can send your worries into Saint Germain's violet flames to be dissolved. This has the effect of setting up events, emotions, and experiences in your life which will actually begin to separate and distance you from your worries. You will be creating the conditions in your life where worry is no longer necessary.

It is not our concern (nor can we know) just how this works. Hilarion is an ascended teacher who has given us the next exercise. You can experience its healing effects if you're willing to give it a try.

 ## Healing Energy

✧ Step One: It is imperative that you practice your meditation daily, and I would prefer that you do some in the morning and some at night. Start out with what is comfortable timing. I know I may sound like a difficult instructor, but there is no time to waste. Begin with at least twenty minutes in the morning and twenty minutes in the evening, and increase this as rapidly as is comfortable for you.

✧ Step Two: When you meditate, breathe. Ask your Higher Self for assistance and instruction that's pertinent to that moment. Constantly be aware of raising your frequency of vibration. Stay relaxed and have a good time.

✧ Step Three: First clean your energies. Look within. Look without. See what is there, and release it. I believe you have a strategy for that already, the "Kiss-It-Goodbye" strategy.

{continued}

✧ Step Four: After cleaning, hang out in bliss! Choose an Ascended Master who appeals to you at the moment and affirm that you are one with that Master. For example, "I am one with Hilarion." Let your active mind repeat the phrase (to keep it busy), and allow your body to become more and more light.

✧ Step Five: The last few minutes of your meditation time, do your healing work and send healing energy where your Higher Self guides you. It may be to people you know, to Earth, to events.

✧ Step Six: When you are through with the healing, give thanks, make your completions, make your separations, and adjust your energy system to be comfortable to interact with other people again.

— Hilarion
channeled by Rev. Cathie Beach

———❧●❧———

Healing Light

Your guides can help you with lightening and releasing your burdens. There are several who are of particular help in the healing process. You might like to call upon Archangel Michael to be with you, to bring his powerful blue sword of Light to sever the karmic ties which are causing your pain, or Saint Germain with his flames of transmutation, or Kuan Yin who gives gentle and loving assistance, or Sananda with healing for the heart.

If you have a goal of healing, you may wish to begin your meditation with affirmations similar to these:

"I release the bondage of pain."

"I no longer create pain for myself or for another."

"I see myself in perfect health and harmony with those around me."

"I joyfully and willingly release and allow the empty space created to be filled with Love and Light."

Much of the work which is done when you call upon the Healing Light or one of the Ascended Masters is nonverbal: it is *energetic*. You will *feel* the healing energies working. You'll feel them running through your body. When the healing is completed, you may feel a lightening or a shift in your energy level. This is probably because some emotional burden has been lifted from you and dissolved.

Pam shares a story of a time when Kuan Yin came to her during meditation: "I was experiencing considerable physical and emotional pain at the time, and I was doing meditation as a part of my daily routine. One evening during the meditation, I heard a voice in my mind saying, 'I am Kuan Yin. I have come to help you with your healing.' She then continued with a beautiful message of how each one of us must first take care of ourselves, that only then can we take care of and teach others. When I told her that I didn't know anything about healing, that I didn't know what to do, she assured me that I should not worry and that she would be helping me. This experience occurred when I first began to channel, so I was quite overwhelmed by it all. I felt intense energy begin to run through my hands as they were guided by the beloved Kuan Yin. She has joined me many times since then, to help with her guidance and healing light, and I am thankful that I have come to know her presence."

Kuan Yin has this message for you:

I come softly and work in gentle ways. My task is to allow people to focus forward, as I help them to release the burdens which keep them looking backwards. They cannot cross over with their head turned or with too much weight. I work more silently than some others, but you can know my presence when you call on me. You will feel my presence as surely as if I was shouting in your ear. You will feel my presence after I have gone as you know a new lightness of being and joy.

You are invited to call upon the loving and gentle assistance of Kuan Yin. She will be there. In a healing meditation, much of the work is done without words. As you sit with the next meditation, be open to the subtle energies and feelings which express themselves. As always, be prepared to record any messages you may receive during or after your healing.

Healing Light

✧ As you sit to begin a healing meditation, allow yourself to become open and receptive to the love pouring down on you from the heavens.

✧ Release the thoughts of the day from your mind and focus on your breath. Breathe complete, full breaths: In ... Out ... . Allow your lungs to fill fully with the breath of life.

✧ Ask for protection and love from the White Light of the Divine Source to surround you.

✧ In your mind, go to your special place where you cannot be disturbed, where there is peacefulness and harmony all around you. Feel the beauty of this place.

✧ Call upon your guides and ask them to help you with the healing you desire. Know that they will come in a very real way and give you this assistance if you truly desire it. One of them in particular may come to you and give you their name or their sign so that you can know their presence.

✧ Now, relax your body. Relax every muscle. Use the "Healing Energy" techniques from the last exercise for recognizing and releasing tension.

{continued}

⬧ See a shaft of White Light pouring down upon your body. This light is full of loving energy.

⬧ Breathe in the Light.

⬧ As you sit in the Light, feel the healing energies as you allow the Light to come in, to fill you and surround you.

⬧ When you are ready, return your attention to the room, feeling a sense of harmony, balance, and love.

The Violet Flame

Much of the healing required for us to become lighter and more filled with love has to do with releasing burdens, attachments, and limitations. Saint Germain is a presence whom you can call upon for assistance in this area. He is well known for the violet ray, or the violet flames of transmutation.

If you have fears, anxieties, or any weight upon your heart, we invite you to open yourself to this healing meditation. It is an exercise for emotional healing. In it, you will call upon Archangel Michael to encircle you with his protective Light. Then you will send Saint Germain all your cares, worries, and concerns. You will send them directly into his violet flames to be dissolved.

You may wish to do the "Healing Energy" work or do the "Healing Light" exercise as a prelude to the "Violet Flames" exercise. You will be lightening your burdens and experiencing the joy that you desire. We are going to visualize together and call upon the Violet Flames.

Violet Flames

◇ Begin your meditation as usual. Concentrate on your breathing and bring yourself to your center.

◇ Think or speak your favorite affirmations:

"I am surrounded by the loving light of Christ."

"I am filled with peace and harmony."

"I am at peace and so attract peace to me."

◇ Visualize a sphere of golden white Light around you as you call upon Saint Germain to be present. Ask Archangel Michael to bring his protective Light to be with you.

◇ Silently affirm within your heart: "I am one with the violet flames." Repeat this to yourself several times until you feel aligned with that statement.

◇ Now, visualize the violet flames filling the entire room. They come from underneath the floor and extend up through the ceiling. Etheric energy is showering down in a gentle, yet penetrating, way to assist you in loosening up and releasing the clouds that are clinging to your emotional bodies.

◇ The violet flames are the antidote to karma. You need not fulfill and live out your karma. You can call upon the violet flames and, by perseverance and acceptance, your karma can be dissolved. This is Grace, a gift that has been given.

◇ Feel your body being filled with beautiful violet flames. Feel them growing and raising your vibrations. You only have to sit and breathe consciously.

◇ Pause and relax.

◇ If you notice that your attention is wandering, you can re-affirm that you are one with the violet flames. This will assist you in maximizing your experience.

{continued}

✧ Connect within yourself, within your emotions or feelings or thoughts, to a certain area in your life in which you desire purification or transmutation, e.g. whatever area is causing you the most difficulty, wherever you feel inertia or limitation.

✧ Begin with just one. Know that you will choose wisely. Think about what it might be and just offer up that area of your life. Hold it within your hands. Simply hold your hands out and visualize yourself releasing that area of your life into an intensification of the Violet Ray.

✧ You may wish to imagine that there is a large bonfire in the middle of the room (or your circle if you are in a group); you can put the thing you wish to release into the fire. You may be a little dramatic doing this if you wish: sweep it into the flames, throw it in, or blow it in with a kiss. However you wish to release it to the flames is all right.

✧ Know that there will be blessings and assistance in this area in your life, as a result of your work.

✧ When you are ready, affirm that you release: "I am releasing _____ (this particular manifestation), finally and completely."

✧ Know, now, that you have placed your pains into the hands of a loving being of light who will dissolve them for you.

✧ So be it.

So, the Violet Flame (or the Violet Ray) is that which will assist you in lightening yourselves, raising the frequency of your vibrations, and removing obstacles. It is very powerful. It may seem subtle to you at first. Be assured that it works, regardless of how powerfully you are able to experience the manifestation. Simply your sincerity in praying and calling for that manifestation is sufficient. You can do this as often as you like. It will not burn you up or burn you out.

When you do the affirmation, "I am one with the Violet Flame," it will assist you in totally surrendering and giving you to this experience. The purity that you achieve will directly enhance your self-mastery and result in your ability to increase the power of your manifestations and fulfill your dreams and desires.

So purify, master, and enjoy the gifts that you have to give yourself and the gifts that we have to share with you, which are many.

— Saint Germain
channeled by Eric Klein

CHAPTER SEVEN

Steps

Now you have the tools to cross the bridge to your own divinity. Given this information and these tools, the big question is "Where do I go from here?" Remember, the purpose of this book is to teach you how to gain your own information and guidance *directly*.

Although we sometimes refer to the ascension as one single event or a series of mass events, it is more importantly a process. The more intensely and faithfully you pursue the ascension process, the more that lightness and loving will become a part of you and the easier your final ascension will be. So preparation is very important. Take the biggest jump, the highest leap, of which you are capable right now.

Ascension is promised in this lifetime for all beings on Earth who desire it. You can experience a "preview" of what it will be like to be ascended, by using the exercises in this chapter. You are already closer to it than you were before you picked up this book. Remember that ascension is a process which you can bring into your daily life. It is a way of being which will surely have an effect on everyone around you. As you become lighter, you will begin to experience joyful changes in your life.

You now have a chance to be closer to the angels. The "Flying with Angels" exercise will give you a chance to take an angelic trip and to telepathically communicate, in love, with another being. This exercise has brought surprising results to many who have tried it. It will be a confirmation to you of your telepathic abilities and will give you a glimmer of the latent potential of your mind.

So, if you feel like floating around a bit, you can try this exercise. Know that you are protected. This exercise was channeled from Archangel Gabriel. We will present it to you unedited, as it was received:

Flying with Angels

To begin, make the usual preparations for meditation. Make yourself comfortable, centered, and protected.

✧ In this exercise, I will be with you and will protect you. If you feel discomfort about flying, you can drop down a silver cord to the Earth and stay anchored. Whatever you are comfortable with is all right.

✧ Just imagine yourself beginning to feel lighter. You can call on me, Archangel Gabriel, or any of the angelic host that you feel an affinity with — your own guardian angel, perhaps.

✧ You are becoming less and less aware of gravity holding you down. You may feel a lightness, a tingling in your legs.

✧ Breathe fully so that you fill your lungs with air.

✧ You may wish to spread your arms out as you visualize your wings unfolding.

{*continued*}

✧ You can go anywhere. You can simply float around this room, if that is comfortable, or you can imagine yourself up above the town where you are, looking down on it. We're together. See the lights getting smaller and smaller as you rise — like being in an airplane, but there is a silence. You can feel the coolness of the winds as you rise, as you drift higher.

✧ Choose a place that you would like to go. If you have someone special whom would like to go to, pay a little visit. You see, you can be like an angel. If there is someone you love and care about, you can take yourself to their town, to their home. Do you see it?

✧ Let's go down and visit them. Make your presence known to this one you love. Let them feel your love. Take all the time you need for this.

✧ If you have a special message for this one, whisper it in their ear. Know that they will hear.

✧ Let the love pour forth from your heart to theirs, for you are with them now in spirit.

✧ When you are ready, you can tell them goodbye. Let them know you are with them and then return back across the distances, however great or small.

✧ See yourself over this town again. And, when you are ready, come back to this room. Come back to your body.

✧ You may find yourself remaining a little light. You may find that you brought a message back with you from the one that you visited.

My heart is full. It was a great joy to take you flying. Know that you can do this anytime on your own. You can be like an angel. You can be close to those that are not near you, and you can speak heart to heart.

— Archangel Gabriel

This exercise can have wonderful results which will let you know that it really worked. Don't be surprised if you get an unexpected visit or hear from the one who received your loving presence in this manner.

As we have progressed along our path, we have had a wonderful teacher: Eric Klein. His task is awakening others to this information. He has been a blessing in our lives and we would like to share with you a meditation he channeled during one of his classes. His books and some tapes of his channeled material are available from Oughten House or through your local New Age bookstore.

Light Pyramids

✧ I would like to ask you to breathe consciously for this guided meditation. I would like you to feel yourself awakening in your higher chakras. We are activating your chakras somewhat.

✧ Maintain your focus on your breath and just feel what you feel. It will be somewhat unique with each of you.

✧ Bring your awareness to the fact that there is a column of light which is passing through each of you into the Earth from above. We are surrounded by this light — protected by it, enlivened by it.

✧ Visualize now, over your heads, a pyramid of light. It is large enough to surround and enclose your entire body. Visualize it descending around you, slowly, until it reaches the floor and closes around you: sealing you, protecting you, filling you with light and peace. I ask you only to sit and breathe and be comfortable in your Light Pyramid. We are working to connect you with your light body.

✧ Meditate silently for a brief time.

{continued}

✧ Visualize the light pyramid rising, slowly and gently, and the column of light returning to its source.

I hope you are enjoying this process, this adventure we are on. You are in for a great deal of joy, of heightened awareness and many miracles. You can visualize this light pyramid in your meditations and affirm for the manifestation of your Light Body. You can use an affirmation such as "I am one with the Light," "I am one with my light body," or any other affirmation which is comfortable to you. But use this technique to work upon bringing down your light body. When you sit beneath this pyramid, you are receiving an enhanced raising of your frequency; much healing will occur. This goes to the deepest level of your beings and it is important work.

— Ashtar
channeled by Eric Klein

In the next exercise you are going to have an opportunity to take a field trip to the fifth dimension. You will be able to experience what it might be like getting there and being there. For the best results, let your imagination allow you to go on this trip. As you gradually bring more light into your body with these exercises, you will actually change your atomic and molecular composition. It then becomes easier to communicate with the Masters and be at home in their world, even if it is only a field trip.

Through the Gate

Remember: the requirements are a *desire* and a *lightness* within your being and within your heart. This is only a field trip, and you may return to your room at any time you desire. Simply ask to return and you will. So, if you are ready to go on a trip, let's begin.

✧ Breathe consciously and be aware of your connection to your Higher Self. See the column of light coming down from above, surrounding and protecting you with love.

✧ Make your affirmations, for example: "I am one with the Light."

✧ Allow your head or arms to move if you wish. You are centered; you are calm; you are relaxed.

✧ Now laugh out loud, "Ha, ha, ha." Let yourself smile and feel the joy of laughter. You must be in a lighthearted state to continue. So, if you feel any heaviness, you can laugh aloud again, feeling the lifting and releasing that laughter brings.

✧ You are sitting comfortably in your chair. You are lightness; you are love; you are a smile. (Are you smiling? Please do!)

✧ Just remain with this feeling of lightness for a few minutes.

✧ Visualize a white dot of energy in the center of the room where you are sitting. Ask your Higher Self to match the frequency of this light for you. This is something your Higher Self can do easily.

✧ Now imagine that the White Light comes toward you and you see that it is a doorway. It is only a few feet in front of you and is wide enough and high enough for you to easily go through. If you do not see the doorway right away, just imagine that it is there.

{continued}

✧ Each person has their own doorway. This is your personal doorway into the fifth dimension, where the Ascended Masters live, where your Higher Self lives. Although this is not an ascension, which will include your physical body, it is a preview of what the ascension will be like. Your physical body will stay in the chair this time, but your mind will take a field trip through the door, then come back to where you started when you are ready to return. Know that you can come back at any time you desire.

✧ Now notice there is someone standing beside the door of light. It is a spiritual being, the Keeper of the Gate, waiting for you. This one is always there by your door, as he or she is for every person. The gatekeeper is waiting for you to laugh and smile. To become lighter, allow yourself to laugh out loud.

✧ Allow the laughter to flow. Release any remaining tension. Feel lighthearted. Be joyful!

✧ Ask the Gatekeeper if you may pass through the door.

✧ Imagine yourself rising off the floor a little and floating slowly towards the door of White Light. Your feet will not serve you here. You must glide foreward slowly, just using your imagination. As you go through, you can feel the presence of the Light around you. It has no temperature but has a slight pressure that is very pleasant.

✧ Feel yourself glide completely through the door. The doorway back to your chair is right behind you. You may return any time you wish.

✧ If you would like to explore a little, you may glide on. You may come to a place where some of the Ascended Masters are waiting to greet you. You may greet them and hug them if you wish. One of the beings you see may be your own Higher Self in its Light Body.

{*continued*}

◇ You may ask questions of any of these beings and may receive direct answers or feelings or impressions. You may stay as long as you like.

◇ Just sit in quiet meditation and enjoy your experiences in the fifth dimension.

◇ When you are ready to return, you may imagine yourself back at the doorway, and you will immediately be there. Just glide back to your chair. You may wish to thank the Keeper of the Gate and your Higher Self for assisting you on your journey.

◇ When you are ready, open your eyes.

For some, the fifth-dimensional field trip, "Through the Gate," brings them into direct contact with their Higher Self, perhaps for the first time. For others, the first contact is more difficult. Just keep practicing!

CHAPTER EIGHT

True Will

We have often asked for guidance concerning our divine paths, and about our missions here on Earth because we both have a desire to be doing work that is fulfilling and meaningful. Sananda is one of the guides who has been a great resource to us. When calling on him one evening, we received this message about these things:

So, you wish guidance on your pathway? Know that you are on it. Although the path is a little rocky at times, know that you are on it. It is enough to know that you are on the path.

When you are hiking in the mountains, you see trail markers — just signposts along the way — to let you know you are on the path. You may have some idea of your destination. You may know it is a particular summit or location, but the path to get you there as you walk over the mountains and through the woods is unknown. You merely see markers along the way and, yes, you know you are on the path. As you trust these markers and continue on, so it is with your life.

Our Higher Self tries to communicate across the gulf that separates it from our conscious self in a variety of ways:

it may come as a hunch or an intuitive feeling; it may be a longing to do or be something different; it may be a talent or an aptitude. To use an older expression, it may be your "calling." However you wish to describe it, we all know when we are doing something that *just feels right.*

Your guides are waiting to support you with your decisions, both large and small, and you are invited to call upon them as you prepare to understand your Divine Path. Know that great assistance and great love are supporting you, and you are not alone — not ever. As you listen to your guidance and come more clearly into touch with your own knowingness, the choices will become more clear and easier to make. It will be clear in every cell of your body when a choice is wrong. It will also be clear in every cell of your body when a choice is right, because the joy and the enthusiasm you feel affirms this for you.

The Divine Path

◇ Start by relaxing and centering yourself as you focus on your breathing. Your breathing can lead you to your center — that calm place within yourself.

◇ Affirm that you are sitting in a space which is safe, which is protected by the Divine Light.

◇ Now, bring some White Light into your heart space. Allow it to grow about you and fill the space that you are in. This is the anchor to your center. It is also the anchor to your highest spiritual guidance.

◇ Be aware of the peace that's in your heart as you call upon Sananda to be with you. Ask Sananda to open your heart and mind to your Higher Self.

{continued}

◇ Affirm that your connection to your Higher Self is clear. It is merged with you. There is no separation. In this space of unity, you know your connection to your own guidance. The channels are strengthened. They are clear and they are strong.

◇ Imagine that the weights are lifted from your feet. The cords of attachment to your burdens are severed so that you may see your path and walk it with a lighter step.

◇ In this space which you have created, put forth the question which is bearing down upon your heart. As you ask your question, be open to receive guidance from the images or messages which come. Ask that the sign be given clearly so that you can recognize its meaning unmistakably.

◇ What are the steps you need to take?

◇ What do you need to release in order to move forward?

◇ Be aware of Sananda's loving presence as you sit in quiet meditation. Know that the answers to your greatest ponderings will become clear to you — if not at this moment, then in the days ahead. Now, come with love in your heart and bring your presence back.

What were your very first thoughts and impressions? You may have received an immediate message. If you didn't, your Higher Self will likely arrange several signals for you during your normal activities in the next few days. Pay particular attention during this time to anything you seem drawn to: a book that may seem to fall off a shelf into your hands, a casual conversation with a friend or acquaintance that seems to strike a chord within you. It may be a new thought that keeps recurring, or one you haven't had in many years. Your Higher Self may try many subtle ways (and perhaps some that aren't so subtle!) to give you the answer.

You might want to repeat this exercise for confirmation. Be particularly aware now how you feel as you go about your daily life. Intensified feelings of enthusiasm or discomfort at this time can be signals in response to your questions during meditation. Remember that you will always have your own free will to make your own choices. What you are asking for is guidance that may help you to get "unstuck," that may help you be brave enough to act upon what you already know. But, when you feel certain that your own free will is in alignment with Divine Will, you will have a sense of the absolute True Will within yourself.

If you think you could consider what your guides are asking you to do, but you have doubts — little nagging concerns, or even big screaming fears — remember that we each have free will. These feelings are your own inner guidance trying to communicate with you.

When you open yourself to receive guidance, it helps you to understand your feelings and to make decisions with additional information. This allows you to be more spontaneous in your decisions. Remember, the decisions are always yours alone to make. No one is ever forced to make a decision they do not wish, for the Masters do not interfere with free will.

Most of us have a tendency to be stuck sometimes and carry on internal dialogues:

"Should I?"

"Yes."

"Should I?"

"No."

If you continue to feel stuck, go back and repeat some of the releasing exercises. You will soon come to know that when your fears and doubts subside, your God-self and spiritual guides will lead you and protect you in ways you could not have imagined. You will know you are on your divine path. This, after all, is why you have an inner God and an inner guide.

Remember that God has arranged all of the circumstances in your universe to be exactly the way they are at exactly this time for a reason known only to Him.

Each person will be presented a view of the choice before them as clearly and in as much detail as they are able to accept. Perhaps other choices will be presented in a sequence, but later choices will depend upon the answers to earlier ones. This is how we strike a balance between forcing your growth a little: by giving you information and opportunities and then waiting to allow you to choose based on what you understand.

You get more choices if you wish more choices. We do not — indeed we cannot — choose for you. We cannot compel you. We cannot even impel you. All we can do is send our messages and illuminate you with our light. But we always allow each being to make his or her own choice.

— Archangel Raphael

If what you find out from doing this exercise is not exactly "news" to you, it's because your Higher Self has been trying to get its message across for a long time. The difference now is that you are consciously paying attention to the message, and perhaps the volume is being "stepped up" a little.

There are many feelings of one kind or another surrounding knowledge of your True Will, especially if money is an issue. We know this firsthand, as writing a book like this was entirely different than running a computer software company, our former occupations. But we were asked to do this project by the Masters in as direct a way as we could imagine: one day there came an inner knowing that we just had to do it. We had the tools, the experience, and were "available." Once we started on this project, we received a lot of assistance from our spiritual guides, and the book is now in your hands.

We do not know where our path may lead us. None of us do. But, we know that we have the very best guidance. We know that the steps we take in the future will be in alignment with our highest good and with our missions here on Earth — that each day will have a purpose. We are aware that we have freedom of choice. The guidance and information that we are receiving will simply make it easier for us to make wise choices.

We are on a grand adventure and wake up each day eager to see what the day will bring to us. As we learn to embrace the Light around and within us, there will be no darkness left. In concrete terms, this means we have no need of fear, resentment or guilt. Negative emotions are the result of seeing ourselves as limited beings. If we could see who we really are, magnificent beings in actuality or potentiality, we would have no desire or need to express any emotions but love, joy, and happiness.

You now have all the tools you need to continue on your path. May your steps be light and your progress swift.

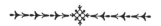

God be with you and near you,
and may you hear Him
loudly and clearly.

⊷ About the Authors ⊶

Fred and Pam are explorers and teachers of self-discovery. They both began channeling messages from the Ascended Masters in 1990. Since that time, they have continued to work closely with their spiritual guidance. They give workshops based on *Bridge Into Light* where their focus is on individual empowerment, by teaching others how to channel information for themselves. In addition to the Ascended Masters, they work with celestial energies and the Ashtar Command. They have also led several groups which worked together, under direct guidance from Spirit, to open a new vortex which is crucial to the Earth's new energy grid.

Fred and Pam have four grown children. They have recently moved from their long-time home in the mountains of California to the high mountains of Colorado. There they continue to channel and write books, produce a bi-monthly newsletter, record meditation tapes, and do world service through their clairvoyant healing work. Pam enjoys working with the devic energies in her garden and Fred's latest project is recording music in their home studio. This music is designed to open our world to frequencies from other realms.

You can find out more about their newsletter, *Light Lines*, and meditation tapes by writing to them c/o Oughten House Publications, P.O. Box 2008, Livermore, CA 94551-2008.

➤➤ About the Artist ◄◄

Reverend Cathie Beach is a clairvoyant artist who enjoys living in Santa Cruz, California. She is becoming well known as an intuitive artist and has drawn the cover art for a number of books. Working closely with each author, she creates art that communicates directly with the intended readership and carries the energy of the book out into a visual representation. Cathie also channels personalized healing drawings which resonate with the individual's energy system in a subtle yet profound way, assisting the process of transformation. You may find out how to contact Cathie through Oughten House Publications.

About the Publisher and Logo

The name "Oughten" was revealed to the publisher fourteen years ago, after three weeks of meditation and contemplation. The combined effect of the letters carries a vibratory signature, signifying humanity's ascension on a planetary level.

The logo represents a new world rising from its former condition. The planet ascends from the darker to the lighter. Our experience of a dark and mysterious universe becomes transmuted by our planet's rising consciousness — glorious and spiritual. The grace of God transmutes the dross of the past into gold, as we leave all behind and ascend into the millennium.

OUGHTEN HOUSE PUBLICATIONS

Our imprint includes books in a variety of fields and disciplines which emphasize the rising planetary consciousness. Literature which relates to the ascension process is our primary line. We are also cultivating a line of thoughtful and beautifully illustrated children's books, which deal with spirituality, angels, mystical realms, and God, the Creator. Our third line of books deals with societal matters, personal growth, poetry, and publications on extraterrestrials.

The list that follows is only a sample of our current offerings. To obtain a complete catalog, contact us at the address shown at the back of this book.

Ascension Books

The Crystal Stair: A Guide to the Ascension, by Eric Klein. — ISBN 1-880666-06-5, $12.95

An Ascension Handbook A practical, in-depth, how-to manual on the ascension process, by Tony Stubbs. — ISBN 1-880666-08-1, $11.95

Bridge Into Light: Your Connection to Spiritual Guidance A how-to book on meditating and channeling, by Pam and Fred Cameron. — ISBN 1-880666-07-3, $11.95

The Inner Door: Channeled Discourses from the Ascended Masters on Self-Mastery and Ascension, by Eric Klein.
Volume One: ISBN 1-880666-03-0, $14.50
Volume Two: ISBN 1-880666-16-2, $14.50

Earth's Birth Changes: St. Germain through Azena A shining new world is coming, channeled by Azena Ramanda. — ISBN 0-646-136-07-0, $19.95

Reality Maintenance 101 Create and maintain your "Christed Reality" by using these prayers and techniques, developed through Commander Augustavia Staresseenia. Item #1002B, $20.00

The Thymus Chakra Handbook A how-to booklet for understanding and using this wonderful chakra. Channeled from The Christ and Kwan Yin by Brenda Montgomery. Item 1004B, $8.50

On Eagle's Wings One of the books recommended in *The Crystal Stair*, this is a collection of communications "from the Universe," given to Ariana over several years. By Ariana Sheran and Friends. Item #1000B, $8.00

E.T. 101 Wit and wisdom to lighten your way on the path, recommended in *The Crystal Stair*. Co-created by Mission Control and Diana Luppi. — ISBN 0-9626958-0-7, $12.00

Other Books for the Rising Planetary Consciousness

Intuition by Design Increase your "Intuition Quotient" through the use of this book and its accompanying set of 36 cards. A valuable tool for applying your intuitive intelligence to all aspects of the decision-making process in your life, by Victor R. Beasley, Ph.D. — ISBN 1-880666-22-7, $15.95

Synergic Power: Beyond Domination, Beyond Permissiveness This book examines the concept of power and how to use power *with* people, not over or against them. By James H. and Marguerite Craig. — ISBN 0-914158-28-7, $8.95

Children's Books

Nature Walk Introducing "Pelfius," the lively little Nature Spirit who lives among the trees, the rivers, and the stars. For children from 2 years and up (adults too!). A beautifully illustrated booklet, by Susan Hays Meredith.
— ISBN 1-880666-09-X, $4.95

Tapes: Discourses and Channeled Material

Ascension Tapes A series of channeled and meditation tapes on the ascension process, by Eric and Christine Klein. Request the list of available tapes from Oughten House.

Bridge Into Light Guides you through the exercises in the book, accompanied by original music composed by Fred Cameron. By Fred and Pam Cameron. Tape #2020T, $9.95

Parallel Realities Learn how to transcend linearity and access your multidimensional nature. By Tashira Tachi-ren. Tape Set #2003T, $44.00

Feminine Aspect of God Mother Mary tells us about her life and the role of women in Jesus' time. Channeled by Crea. Tape 2013T, $8.95

Extraterrestrial Vision, Vols. 1, 2, and 3 The history of the human race, the role of extraterrestrials in our history, how to tell positive ETs from negative ones, and what is coming in our future. The mid-causal entity Theodore, channeled by Gina Lake. Tapes #2010T, #2011T, and #2012T, $9.95 each.

Birthing the Era of God The music of Michael Hammer accompanies this guided meditation from The Divine Mother, channeled by Claire Heartsong. Tape #2017T, $13.00

Preparation for Ascension, #1 The I AM presence of Yeshua Sananda facilitates our ascension process with limitless love. Channeled by Claire Heartsong. Tape #2018T, $13.00

Other Tapes

Mary's Lullaby A healing meditation sent to us by Mary, Mother of Jesus. A soothing melody, combined with the angelic voice of Claire Applegate. Tape #5007T, $9.95

Song of Gothar A story of deep emotional healing, when the longings of the heart are given voice. By Deborah Nayanna Barrable. Tape #5013T, $12.95

The Yogi from Muskogee, Don't Squeeze the Shaman, and **Enlightening Strikes Again** Famed entertainer Swami Beyondananda puts *fund*amental before *trance*ndental. A welcome break for comic relief on the spiritual path. Tapes #6002T, #6003T, and #6004T, $11.00 each.

Products

Ascension Cards A collection of over 50 quotations and messages, selected from various books published by Oughten House. These cards may serve as a source of daily inspiration and to help one focus on one's own ascension process. They may also serve as a beautiful gift item for a friend or loved one. (Details in catalog)

Music Tapes and CDs

EL AN RA A beautiful piece of ascension music, to raise you to new levels of bliss. By Stefan Jedland. Tape #5017T, $11.95

Awakening Six lovely compositions embodying ascension energies through the voices of piano, strings, bells, and flutes. By Brad C. Rudé. Tape #5003T, $8.95

Tales from the Future One of the *Inner Landscapes* series by Michael Pollack, a best-seller defined as "music for the next generation after ascension." Tape #5014T, $10.99; CD #5018CD, $15.99

Call of the Heart This special album of vocal and instrumental music arose from communing with God and nature. By Greg Gille. Tape #5006T, $10.95

Angels in the Rain Randall Leonard's original piano solos. Beautiful and relaxing music, recommended by Louise L. Hay. Tape #5000T, $10.00

Awake, Arise, Ascend Connie Stardancer's heartfelt singing, accompanied by Richard Shulman's exquisite musical arrangements. Tape #5012T, $10.00

A Higher Dimension Created near Mt. Shasta by Richard Shulman, these tranquil solo piano pieces inspire meditation, realxation, and healing. Tape #5010T, $10.00

READER NETWORKING AND MAILING LIST

The ascension process presents itself as a new dimension and reality for many of us on Planet Earth. Oughten House Publications now stands in the midst of many Starseeds and Lightworkers who seek to know more. Thousands of people worldwide are reaching out to find others of like mind and to network with them.

You have the opportunity to stay informed and be on our networking mailing list. Send us the enclosed Information Reply Card or a letter. We will do our best to keep you and your network of friends up to date with ascension-related literature, materials, author tours, workshops, and channelings.

If you have a network database or small mailing list you would like to share, please send it along.

CATALOG REQUESTS

&

BOOK ORDERS

Catalogs will gladly be sent upon request. Book orders must be prepaid: check, money order, international coupon, VISA, MasterCard accepted. Include shipping and handling (US postal book rate): $3.50 first book; add 50¢ for each additional book. Send orders to:

OUGHTEN HOUSE PUBLICATIONS
P.O. Box 2008
Livermore • California • 94551-2008 • USA
Phone (510) 447-2332
Fax (510) 447-2376